Dion Boucicault

London assurance. A comedy in five Acts

2. Band

Dion Boucicault

London assurance. A comedy in five Acts
2. Band

ISBN/EAN: 9783744789318

Printed in Europe, USA, Canada, Australia, Japan

Cover: Foto ©Thomas Meinert / pixelio.de

More available books at **www.hansebooks.com**

LONDON ASSURANCE.

A Comedy,

IN FIVE ACTS.

BY DION L. BOUCICAULT,

Author of "The Shaugraun," "Love in a Maze," "The Octoroon," "Our American Cousin," "The Colleen Bawn," "Arrah-na-Pogue," etc., etc.

AS FIRST PRODUCED AT COVENT GARDEN THEATRE, LONDON, IN 1841, AND AT THE PARK THEATRE, NEW YORK, OCT. 11 OF THE SAME YEAR.

AN ENTIRELY NEW ACTING EDITION.

WITH FULL STAGE DIRECTIONS—CAST OF CHARACTERS—SYNOPSIS OF SCENERY—FULL DESCRIPTION OF COSTUMES EXPRESSLY COMPILED FOR THIS WORK—STORY OF THE PLAY—REMARKS—NOTES, ETC.

EDITED BY

ALFRED B. SEDGWICK,

Author of "Leap Year," "The Twin Sisters," "The Queerest Courtship," "My Walking Photograph," "Sold Again and Got the Money," "Circumstances Alter Cases," etc., etc., etc.

———◆———

NEW YORK:
CLINTON T. DE WITT, PUBLISHER,
No. 33 ROSE STREET.
(BETWEEN DUANE AND FRANKFORT STREETS.)

CAST OF CHARACTERS.

	Covent Garden, London, 1841.	Park Theatre, N. Y., 1841.	Bowery Theatre, 1842.	Broadway Theatre, 1848.
Sir Harcourt Courtley	Mr. W. Farren.	Mr. Placide.	Mr. W. Blake.	Mr. W. Blake.
Charles Courtley	Mr. Anderson.	Mr. Wheatley.	Mr. Abbott.	Mr. G. Vandenhoff.
Dazzle	Mr. Charles Matthews.	Mr. Browne.	Mr. Hamblin.	Mr. Lester.
Max Harkaway	Mr. Bartley.	Mr. Fisher.	Mr. J. Gilbert.	
Dolly Spanker	Mr. Keeley.	Mr. W. H. Williams.	Mr. W. A. Chapman	Mr. Dawson.
Mark Meddle	Mr. Harley.	Mr. Latham.	Mr. Gates.	
Cool	Mr. Brindal.	Mr. A. Andrews.	Mr. Foster.	
Solomon Isaacs				
Martin	Mr. Ayliffe.	Mr. Howard.		
Simpson (Butler)	Mr. Honner.	Mr. King.		
Lady Gay Spanker	Mrs. Nesbett.	Miss Charlotte Cushman.	Mrs. Shaw.	Miss Fanny Wallack.
Grace Harkaway	Madame Vestris.	{ Miss Clarendon. / Miss Buloid. }	Mrs. Herring.	Miss Rose Telbin.
Pert	Mrs. Humby.	Mrs. Vernon.	Miss Clarke.	

	Burton's Chambers st. 1849.	Niblo's, 1858.	Laura Keene's, 1858.	Wallack's, 1876.
Sir Harcourt Courtley	A Southern Amateur.	Mr. Placide.	Mr. J. S. Browne.	Mr. John Gilbert.
Charles Courtley				Mr. H. J. Montague.
Dazzle	Mr. John Brougham.	Mr. John Brougham.	Mr. C. M. Walcot.	Mr. Lester Wallack.
Max Harkaway	Mr. Lynne.			Mr. J. W. Shannon.
Dolly Spanker	Mr. Redmond Ryan.			Mr. W. R. Floyd.
Mark Meddle	Mr. Burton.	Mr. Blake.		Mr. Harry Beckett.
Cool				Mr. E. M. Holland.
Solomon Isaacs				Mr. J. Peck.
Martin				Mr. J. F. Josephs.
Simpson (Butler)				
Lady Gay Spanker	Miss Fanny Wallack.	Miss Charlotte Cushman.		Miss Ada Dyas.
Grace Harkaway	Miss Taylor.			Miss Ione Burke.
Pert				Miss Effie Germon.

SYNOPSIS OF SCENERY.

ACT I.
Reception-Room in Sir HARCOURT's House, London.

ACT II.
Manor-House and Grounds, Oak Hall, Gloucestershire.

ACTS III., IV. AND V.
Drawing-Room and Boudoir in Oak Hall.

TIME OF REPRESENTATION—TWO HOURS AND FORTY-FIVE MINUTES.

ACT I.—Vestibule Interior. Brown striped wainscoting.

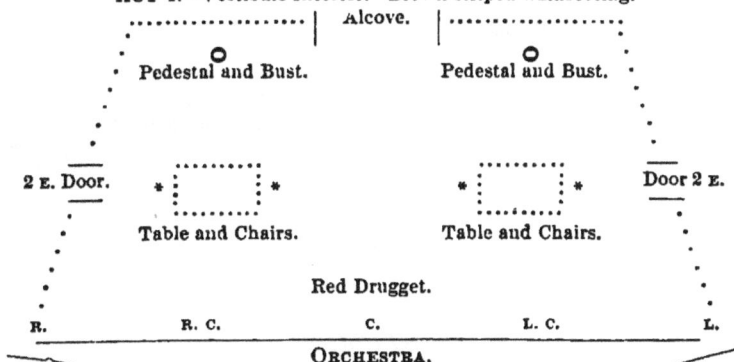

.... | Alcove. | ....

O

Pedestal and Bust.   Pedestal and Bust.

2 E. Door.   * [: Table and Chairs. :] *   * [: Table and Chairs. :] *   Door 2 E.

Table and Chairs.   Table and Chairs.

Red Drugget.

R.   R. C.   C.   L. C.   L.

ORCHESTRA.

ACT II.—Park Exterior. Light wood and distant road.
Backing.

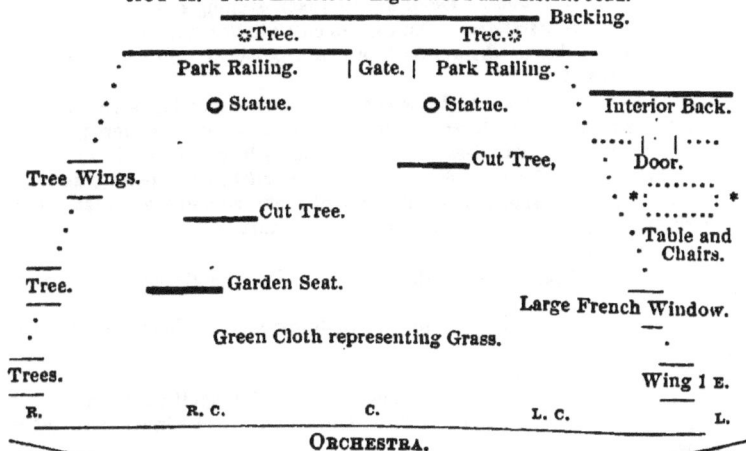

⚬Tree.   Tree.⚬

Park Railing. | Gate. | Park Railing.

O Statue.   **O** Statue.   Interior Back.

——Cut Tree,   Door.

Tree Wings.

——Cut Tree.   * [:] * Table and Chairs.

Tree.

——Garden Seat.

Large French Window.

Green Cloth representing Grass.

Trees.

Wing 1 E.

R.   R. C.   C.   L. C.   L.

ORCHESTRA.

ACTS III., IV. and V.—Half-flat representing interior of Drawing-room. Handsome crimson furniture.

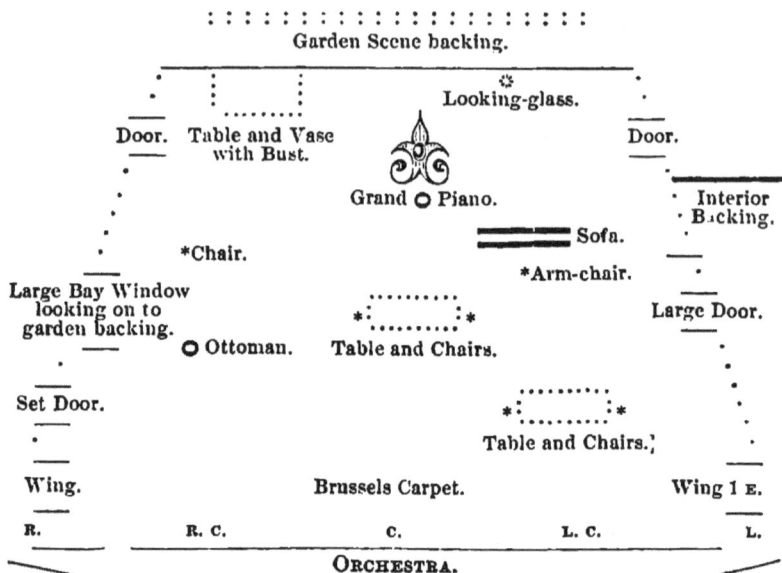

: :
Garden Scene backing.

Looking-glass.

Door.   Table and Vase   Door.
with Bust.

Grand ○ Piano.   Interior
Backing.

Sofa.

*Chair.   *Arm-chair.

Large Bay Window
looking on to   Large Door.
garden backing.
○ Ottoman.   Table and Chairs.

Set Door.   Table and Chairs.

Wing.   Brussels Carpet.   Wing 1 E.

R.   R. C.   C.   L. C.   L.

ORCHESTRA.

COSTUMES.

SIR HARCOURT COURTLEY.—*First dress:* Handsome brocaded dressing-gown; embroidered slippers; silk stockings; gold embroidered cap; dark curly wig, etc. *Second dress:* Black frock coat and trousers; white vest; high black stock and stand-up collar. *Third dress:* Black evening suit.

CHARLES COURTLEY.—*First dress:* Dark green coat; light pants; dark vest; cloak with pockets. *Second dress:* Dark-brown frock-coat. *Third dress:* Fashionable black suit.

MAX HARKAWAY.—*First dress:* Dark coat, cut in the sporting style of a rich country gentleman; white vest; black pants; drab, high gaiters; walking-stick; gray wig. *Second dress:* Old gentleman's black dress-suit.

DAZZLE.—*First dress:* Green fashionable cut-away coat; drab pants; dark vest. *Second dress:* The same, with addition of light summer overcoat. *Third dress:* Blue dress-coat; brass buttons; black pants.

MEDDLE.—Dark clerical suit.

DOLLY SPANKER.—*First dress:* Dark-blue coat; check pants and vest. *Second dress:* Black evening-suit.

COOL.—*First dress:* Light coat; white vest; black pants. *Second dress:* Black suit.

SERVANTS.—Undress livery.

LADY GAY SPANKER.—*First dress:* Crimson velvet riding habit; gentleman's high hat; green veil; riding whip. *Second dress:* Genteel dinner dress of the period.

GRACE HARKAWAY.—*First dress:* Fashionable white muslin morning-dress. *Second dress:* Fashionable dinner costume.

PERT.—Neat dark merino dress; ribbons; white apron.

PROPERTIES.

ACT I.—Knocker and bell for prompter ; table and chairs R. and L., covered ; knockers and broken bell-pulls for CHARLES COURTLEY to produce from pocket ; cards on tray, and hand-bell on table, R. H. ; drugget for floor.

ACT II.—Flowers in pot, practicable, to pluck, and garden chairs ; written paper ; note book with leaf to tear out, and pencil for DAZZLE ; green carpet down to represent lawn.

ACT III.—Chintz furniture ; table and two chairs, R. C., well down ; ottoman R. C. ; grand piano and stool at back, sofa near it, L. C. ; table and two chairs, C., with flowers, etc. ; chairs spread in other parts of the room ; writing materials and candelabra with lighted candles on table C. ; riding-whip for LADY GAY SPANKER ; dinner bell for prompter ; folded letter for COOL ; pocket-book and stamped acceptance for DAZZLE ; chess-board and chess-men on table, L. C. ; arm-chair L. C. 2 E. ; small table backed by gilt mirror, with vase and bust on it, against flat, L. C. ; Brussels carpet.

ACT IV.—Furniture, etc., same as Act III.; smelling-bottle for SIR HARCOURT ; dinner-bell for prompter.

ACT V.—Two sure-firing pistols, at L. 1 E. ; writing material , red sealing-wax and lighted taper on table, C.; cigars in cigar-case, for DAZZLE.

EXPLANATION OF THE STAGE DIRECTIONS.

The Actor is supposed to face the Audience.

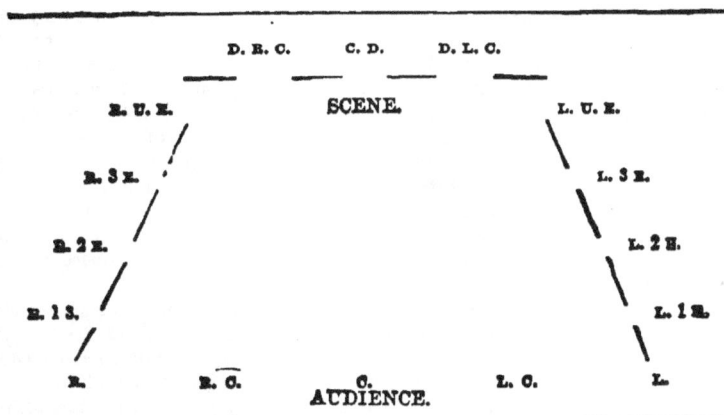

L.	Left.	
L. C.	Left Centre.	
L. 1 E.	Left First Entrance.	
L. 2 E.	Left Second Entrance.	
L. 3 E.	Left Third Entrance.	
L. U. E.	Left Upper Entrance (wherever this Scene may be.)	
D. L. C.	Door Left Centre.	

C.	Centre.
R.	Right.
R. 1 E.	Right First Entrance.
R. 2 E.	Right Second Entrance.
R. 3 E.	Right Third Entrance.
R. U. E.	Right Upper Entrance.
D. R. C.	Door Right Centre.

SYNOPSIS.

THOSE who attend a performance of "London Assurance " at the present day, will scarcely realize it as being an accurate photograph of the current "outside" ways and manners of Londoners between the years 1835 to 1840. Those times when the late eccentric Marquis of Waterford ruled supreme-as chief spirit of all the follies of the day.

CHARLES COURTLEY, a young man of fashion, and a collegian on vacation— (those who have read " Tom Brown at Oxford " will readily understand the character)—has been on a "spree." He has picked up—or rather has been picked up by a quondam acquaintance—one DAZZLE, whom he has no recollection of having seen before, and probably never had. Mr. DAZZLE is a man about town. He cuts a respectable appearance, and having no apparent means of living, manages to make an apparently respectable living—without means. Everybody seems to tolerate him, but no one knows who he is, or where he came from. DAZZLE is— DAZZLE, who having with much trouble and ingenuity managed to entice CHARLES COURTLEY home at about half-past nine in the morning, much to the discontent of the sleepy servants, who have been waiting up all night for him, to hide his indiscretions from his father, before that venerable dandy, who is undoubtedly the fashionable scoundrel of the play, shall have rung the bell for his morning chocolate. Not that they are at all pleased to find him brought home in so very dilapidated condition by a stranger, or to see him produce broken knockers and bell-handles from his pockets as trophies of success. But as there is no time to lose, they, with the assistance of DAZZLE, manage to get him to bed before the entrance of SIR HARCOURT ; who, whatever he may be himself, holds firm conviction in the strict morality of his son.

SIR HARCOURT COURTLEY, though now over sixty, still imagines himself a young man, and a handsome one at that. A spendthrift in his youth, he has been the victim of an old friend, a Mr. Harkaway, who advanced him heavy sums of money, taking as security mortgages on the Courtley property. To use his own words, " being a penurious, miserly, ugly old scoundrel, he made a market of my indiscretion, and supplied my extravagance with large sums of money on mortgages, his great desire being to unite the two properties. About seven years ago he died, leaving GRACE, his daughter, to the guardianship of her uncle, with this will : If on attaining the age of nineteen she would consent to marry me, I should receive those deeds and all his property as her dowry. If she refused to comply with this condition, they should revert to my heir, presumptive or apparent. She consents. I consent to receive her £15,000 a year."

Thus we see him, with almost one foot in the grave, preparing to commit matrimony, although he has never seen the lady since her childhood, having lived on the Continent seven years previous to the opening of the play. While so engaged he is visited by Squire MAX HARKAWAY, GRACE's uncle and guardian, a bluff, hearty, honest fox hunter, who thinks more of a brisk chase than of all the fashionable follies of the day put together. He is opposed to the match, but has no power to prevent it ; and it is finally agreed that they shall go down to MAX's seat in Gloucestershire, together, in order that SIR HARCOURT may be introduced to GRACE. SIR HARCOURT retires to prepare his toilet (a ceremony which with him supersedes all others), leaving HARKAWAY to await his return. While so doing he encounters DAZZLE, who has managed to get CHARLES to lie down. Taken by his off-hand manner, and presuming, from finding him making so free in the house, that he must be an intimate friend of the family, MAX cordially invites DAZZLE to join the party at Oak Hall. DAZZLE of course accepts at once. It would be against his interest to refuse. SIR HARCOURT and Squire HARKAWAY depart for Gloucestershire, and later in the day, CHARLES, having slept off the effects of his last night's debauch, and finding DAZZLE making himself quite at home, orders the servants to show him the door. But DAZZLE wont go. He has once got his foot in the Courtley mansion, and means to keep it there. He reproaches CHARLES with ingratitude, and to show that he is above petty malice, he in the coolest manner actually invites him down to his country house. "Oak Hall, Gloucestershire." CHARLES, who has been kept at school or college all his life, knows nothing of the Harkaways, and as he is beset by duns and sheriff's officers, he, to avoid one of the most persistent, a Mr. SOLOMON ISAACS, who is then waiting in the hall for him, jumps at the chance, and off they go, escaping through the stables, on their jouney to Gloucestershire.

The second Act opens at the house and grounds of Squire HARKAWAY. GRACE is momentarily expecting the return of her uncle, accompanied by SIR HARCOURT. She is a country girl, who has never seen the world, never had an *affaire de cour*, knows nothing of love, has no objection to marry a man she has never seen, and who is nearly old enough to be her grandfather, and looks on marriage as a mere mercantile transaction. We are here introduced to a personage who is mixed up with all the other characters of the piece to a considerable extent during the rest of the action, one Mr. MARK MEDDLE, a pettifogging country lawyer, who is always poking his nose into other people's business, in hope of obtaining a fee. He has just discovered the news of the approaching wedding through the columns of the village newspaper, and is fishing for spoils. To draw up the marriage contract would be the acme of professional bliss, and he has called at the Hall to pump the servants, but they are not to be pumped. DAZZLE and CHARLES have just arrived, and DAZZLE meeting MEDDLE on the lawn, mistakes him for one of the family, and immediately begins to cultivate his acquaintance. MEDDLE, nothing loath, reciprocates, and they are getting on remarkably well, when CHARLES, who while walking through the grounds has caught a glimpse of GRACE and fallen desperately in love at first sight, enters, and is immediately introduced to the lawyer by DAZZLE, as his very old friend, Mr. MEDDLE, while he introduces CHARLES as "Mr. Augustus Hamilton." DAZZLE having discovered GRACE's name, hurries off to introduce himself, when a comical scene ensues between MEDDLE and young COURTLEY.

MEDDLE, afterwards seeing the future Lady Courtley and "Mr. Augustus Hamilton" in close conversation, hides behind a tree to take notes in the event of a future "Crim. Con." case. CHARLES, who is likewise only known to GRACE by the name of Hamilton, enters into a desperate flirtation with her, when he discovers that she is about to be married—but not to whom ? They are interrupted by a servant announcing the return of MAX HARKAWAY, accompanied by an unknown gentleman, whom GRACE hastens to greet as her future husband. CHARLES, anxious to find out whether there is any truth in GRACE's statement, as also the name of the bridegroom, consults MEDDLE, but that wily gentleman can impart no intelligence without a heavy fee. Baffled here, he hastens to call on DAZZLE to assist him.

Meanwhile GRACE has been introduced to SIR HARCOURT, and DAZZLE has been welcomed by MAX, to whom he has introduced CHARLES as his particular friend, "Augustus Hamilton." And now comes one of the strongest situations in the play, the meeting between father and son, and the denial of his father's identity by that son.

MAX, in his bluff country hospitality, hastens to introduce the two young men to SIR HARCOURT COURTLEY, who of course, with the greatest possible surprise, instantly recognizes his own offspring, although the old gentleman is considerably ashamed of having to own to so old a son. CHARLES, in his confusion, by advice of DAZZLE, denies being Charles Courtley—or even knowing such a person. SIR HARCOURT, in amazement, calls on his valet COOL as a witness. But this personage, true to his name, as coolly denies his young master. "No, sir ; it is not Mr. Charles—but it is very like him !" A short dispute follows, urged on by MEDDLE, who would like to be retained for an action, when luncheon is announced—that great pacificator of angry passion—and all retire save MEDDLE and COOL, who have a very funny little interview, which terminates the Act.

A lapse of two days has taken place between the second and third Acts, and we find the parties seated in MAX HARKAWAY's drawing-room, GRACE and CHARLES being engaged in a game of chess. SIR HARCOURT is full of angry suspicion. He looks on CHARLES and DAZZLE as a pair of swindlers, and has written up to London ordering his son's instant appearance at Oak Hall. The cool, impudent manner in which DAZZLE treats the baronet, is fanning a flame in the breast of the haughty old coxcomb, that is not a little heightened by the evident flirtation amounting to love passages that are still being kept up between CHARLES and SIR HARCOURT's intended bride, when Mr. ADOLPHUS and LADY GAY SPANKER appear on the scene. LADY GAY SPANKER! Who and what is she? " Glee! glee! made a living thing! Nature in some frolic mood, shut up a merry devil in her eye, and spiting Art stole Joy's bright harmony to thrill her laugh, which peals out sorrow's knell. Her cry rings loudest in the field—the very echo loves it best, and as each hill attempts to ape her voice, earth seems to laugh that it made a thing so glad."

LADY GAY is an Earl's daughter. As MAX HARKAWAY very tersely puts it, "she married Dolly for freedom, he—her for protection, and he has it!" In fact DOLLY is an eccentric little gentleman, and as may well be supposed, of means. He is little better than a fool, but very fond of his "field sport" loving wife. Nevertheless, he is a gentleman, which some actors of the part have forgotten to perceive. He is exceedingly nervous, depending on his wife for advice in everything. He is even afraid to enter the room at the same time that his wife rushes in brimful of youthful spirits, fresh and blooming from her morning ride over the stone fences of Gloucestershire, and ready to devour her dear cousin GRACE and her "dear old papa," as she calls MAX, with kisses. The baronet, who is smitten at once, to the evident amazement of DAZZLE, who now remains a quiet looker-on, wonders (after LADY GAY has laughingly refused his escort to GRACE's apartments, where she will dress for dinner, and has run off to them alone), how it was possible that "Dolly ever summoned courage to propose." "Bless you, he never did," returns HARKAWAY. "She proposed to him. She says—he would, if he could! but as he couldn't—she did for him."

COOL, in meantime, has intercepted SIR HARCOURT's London message, and now comes to inform his young master. He luckily finds him alone with DAZZLE. CHARLES is distracted and cannot possibly tear himself away from GRACE, but DAZZLE, ever ready for emergencies, and knowing how SIR HARCOURT is set on the conquest of DOLLY SPANKER's protectress, forms a plan by which he can, with the aid of that lady, make SIR HARCOURT readily consent to his son's marriage with Squire HARKAWAY's ward and niece. He first assures COOL that Mr. CHARLES COURTLEY will be on hand in person at the appointed time ; and then proceeds to tackle SIR HARCOURT, whose mental thought as he approaches, amounts to " Here's that cursed fellow again !" DAZZLE has a secret of importance to disclose to him, and an amusing scene ensues, wherein he tickles the old gentleman's vanity, by warning him against the seductive society of LADY SPANKER. At first he is offended, but when DAZZLE assures him that he is a distant relative of the Spankers, he is dumbfounded, and thinks he must be related to every distinguished family in Great Britain. DAZZLE persuades him that LADY GAY has been much struck with his address ; that she has evidently laid herself out for display, in an endeavor to entangle him, till the baronet is in ecstacy at his good fortune. Of course he promises all that DAZZLE requires, mentally resolving to do nothing of the kind but to effect an easy conquest. They become mutually confidential. DAZZLE assures him that the way in which he met Mr. MAX HARKAWAY in Belgrave square, was through his son's charitable disposition. He held an acceptance of his for £100, with which CHARLES had relieved a poor man with a large family ; and he actually wheedles the money out of the old man to pay the imaginary debt, first obtaining CHARLES' endorsement to half a dozen notes, for which he has "stamped" blanks conveniently ready in his pocket-book, while assuring the younger COURTLEY that he ought to be glad to find a friend who not only gives him good advice, but finds him money as well.

Soon after GRACE and CHARLES meet. A mutual understanding and a declaration take place, and he is in the act of folding her in his arms, when LADY GAY suddenly surprises them. GRACE runs away in terrible confusion. CHARLES makes LADY SPANKER his confidant ; tells her who he really is, and asks her assistance. She falls readily and merrily into the plot against SIR HARCOURT—but how about SPANKER ? He might object ? Oh ! he's an estimable little character. He could not possibly have any objection—and so my lady commences her work at the dinner-table.

The fourth and fifth Acts are necessary to the development of the plot against SIR HARCOURT. After dinner the ladies retire, while the gentlemen, as usual in those days, remain to discuss politics or otherwise chat over their wine. GRACE receives a note from "Hamilton," renouncing her, and saying that he has left for London, which nearly makes her faint, or at least pretend to ; but he soon turns up again in his real character of CHARLES HARCOURT. She sees through the *ruse*, and there is considerable love sparring between them. Meanwhile DOLLY has taken a little too much wine at the table, and has become brave. He wants to assert his rights as a man and a husband, to the extreme secret delight of LADY GAY, who dearly loves him. Still, knowing the position that both CHARLES and GRACE are in, she carries on her flirtation with SIR HARCOURT, till he actually proposes an elopement. MEDDLE has been watching and interfering with everybody. He watches CHARLES and GRACE, LADY GAY and the baronet. He informs DOLLY of the intended elopement, who gets violently jealous and challenges SIR HARCOURT. The duel is, however, stopped by MAX, through information from LADY SPANKER, who fears for her husband's life, and feels that she has gone too far. CHARLES is arrested by Mr. SOLOMON ISAACS, and thus his father is assured that "Mr. Augustus Hamilton" and his son are one and the same person. GRACE pays the debt, at the same time offering her hand and fortune to CHARLES COURTLEY. SIR HARCOURT, finding that he has made a preposterous fool of himself in his old age, graciously consents. DOLLY and LADY SPANKER have come to an understanding, and feel happier with each other than ever before, while everybody is anxious to find out who DAZZLE is. The substance of his reply is—"that Dazzle *is* Dazzle !—and no one else."

The comedy ends with a tag, which placed in the mouth of SIR HARCOURT COURTLEY, is preposterous, as it consists of moral advice to his son.

REMARKS

THE comedy of "London Assurance" was first produced in America at the old Park Theatre, Oct. 11, 1847, with an attention to scenery, furniture and appointments hitherto unattempted on our stage. Quoting from Ireland's Records of the New York Stage, page 367, vol. 2, we find that in SIR HARCOURT COURTLEY, Mr. Placide made an impression unequalled by any successor, and to this day is the only acknowledged representative of the part. Browne was accused of overdoing DAZZLE, and dressed the character very shabbily, but his spirit and brazen assurance were so much in keeping with its requirements, that over-nice critics alone condemned him. LADY GAY SPANKER was the first original character in high comedy in which Miss Charlotte Cushman made a decided hit, but she also was liable to the charge of overacting, a charge which did not justly lie at the door of Miss Clarendon, engaged expressly for GRACE HARKAWAY, for she unfortunately scarcely acted at all, and after a few nights was withdrawn, and Miss Buloid substituted. Wheatley made the best CHARLES COURTLEY, and Andrews the most perfect Cool, that have ever been seen in New York. Notwithstanding the slight objections in the cast, " London Assurance " was the most popular play of the season, during which it was performed nearly fifty times. We next hear of its being produced at the New Chatham, on the 9th of May, 1842, Mr. Lambert being expressly engaged for Sir Harcourt, Mrs. Blake performing Lady Gay ; and at the Bowery under Mr. Hamblin's management, on the same evening, with Mr. Blake, Mr. Gilbert and Mrs. Shaw in the cast.

It was again produced in New York at the Broadway Theatre, corner of Pearl and Anthony (now Worth) streets, then in the first season of its career, March 1, 1848, with Mr. J. Lester Wallack (then acting under the name of Lester), as Dazzle, Mr. Blake as Sir Harcourt, G. Vandenhoff as Charles, Miss Fanny Wallack as Lady Gay, and Miss Rose Telbin as Grace.

Mr. Burton afterwards produced this comedy at his little theatre in Chambers street, July 16, 1849, with the first appearance of a " Southern gentleman amateur " as Sir Harcourt, Burton himself taking the part of Meddle, while Mr. John Brougham was cast for Dazzle.

We find that it was afterwards produced at Wallack's old theatre (corner of Broome street and Broadway, now pulled down) at its re-opening under Mr. W. Stuart's management, on the 3d of September, 1857, with Mr. and Mrs. John Wood, Walcot, Blake, Boucicault, Lester Wallack, Miss Agnes Robertson and Miss Mary Gannon in the cast ; it having been previously acted at Niblo's, on the 28th of June in the same year, on which occasion Miss Charlotte Cushman once more resumed the *rôle* of Lady Gay, Placide, Brougham and Blake assisting her. It was again repeated at Laura Keene's, Oct. 4, 1858, with the veteran J. S. Browne as Sir Harcourt, and C. M. Walcot as Dazzle.

Of the early casts in America, C. Wheatley, Blake, Abbott, Hamblin, W. A. Chapman, Placide, Lynn, Burton, J. S. Brown, Walcot, Charlotte Cushman, Mrs. Shaw, Helen Taylor, Mary Gannon and others have all passed away, and Lester Wallack, the génial John Brougham, and Mr. Gilbert are, among the privileged few left " to tell the tale."

" 'Tis true—'tis pity ! Pity 'tis—'tis true."

Alfred B. Sedgwick.

LONDON ASSURANCE.

ACT I.

SCENE.—*An ante-room* in Sir Harcourt Courtley's *house in Belgrave square.*

Enter Cool, c.

Cool. Half-past nine, and Mr. Charles has not yet returned. I am in a fever of dread. If his father happens to rise earlier than usual on any morning, he is sure to ask first for Mr. Charles. Poor deluded old gentleman—he little thinks how he is deceived.

Enter Martin, *lazily,* L.

Well, Martin, he has not come home yet!
Martin. No; and I have not had a wink of sleep all night. I cannot stand this any longer; I shall give warning. This is the fifth night Mr. Courtley has remained out, and I'm obliged to stand at the hall window to watch for him.
Cool. You know, if Sir Harcourt was aware that we connived at his son's irregularities, we should all be discharged.
Mar. I have used up all my common excuses on his duns. "Call again," "Not at home," and "Send it down to you," won't serve any more; and Mr. Crust, the wine merchant, swears he will be paid.
Cool. So they all say. Why, he has arrests out against him already. I've seen the fellows watching the door. (*loud knock and ring heard*) There he is, just in time—quick, Martin, for I expect Sir William's bell every moment, (*bell rings*) and there it is. [*Exit* Martin, *slowly.*
Thank Heaven! he will return to college to-morrow, and this heavy responsibility will be taken off my shoulders. A valet is as difficult a post to fill properly as that of prime minister. [*Exit,* L.
Young C. (*without*). Hollo?
Dazzle (*without*). Steady!

Enter Young Courtley *and* Dazzle, L.

Young C. Hollo-o-o!
Daz. Hush! what are you about, howling like a Hottentot. Sit down there, and thank Heaven you are in Belgrave square instead of Bow street.
Young C. D—d—d—n Bow street.
Daz. Oh, with all my heart!—you have not seen as much of it as I have.
Young C. I say—let me see—what was I going to say?—oh, look

here—(*pulls out a large assortment of bell-pulls, knockers, etc., from his pocket*) There! dam'me! I'll puzzle the two-penny postmen—I'll deprive them of their right of disturbing the neighborhood. That black lion's head did belong to old Vampire, the money-lender; this bell-pull to Miss Stitch, the milliner.

Daz. And this brass griffin——

Young C. That! oh, let me see—I think I twisted that off our own hall-door as I came in, while you were paying the cab.

Daz. What shall I do with them?

Young C. Pack 'em up in a hamper, and send 'em to the sitting magistrate with my father's compliments; in the meantime come into my room, and I'll astonish you with some Burgundy.

Re-enter Cool, l. c.

Cool (r.) Mr Charles——

Young C. Out! out! not at home to any one.

Cool. And drunk——

Young C. As a lord.

Cool. If Sir Harcourt knew this, he would go mad, he would discharge me.

Young C. You flatter yourself; that would be no proof of his insanity. (*to* Dazzle) This is Cool, sir, Mr. Cool; he is the best liar in London—there is a pungency about his invention, and an originality in his equivocation, that is perfectly refreshing.

Cool (*aside*). Why, Mr. Charles, where did you pick him up?

Young C. You mistake, he picked *me* up. (*bell rings.*)

Cool. Here comes Sir Harcourt—pray do not let him see you in this state.

Young C. State! what do you mean? I am in a beautiful state.

Cool. I should lose my character.

Young C. That would be a fortunate epoch in your life, Cool.

Cool. Your father would discharge me.

Young C. Cool, my dad is an old ass.

Cool. Retire to your own room, for Heaven's sake, Mr. Charles.

Young C. I'll do it for my own sake. (*to* Dazzle) I say, old fellow, (*staggering*) just hold the door steady while I go in. .

Daz. This way. Now, then!—take care!

[*Helps him into the room,* r.

Enter Sir Harcourt Courtley, l. c., *in an elegant dressing-gown, and Greek skull-cap and tassels, etc.*

Sir Harcourt. Cool, is breakfast ready?

Cool. Quite ready, Sir Harcourt.

Sir H. Apropos. I omitted to mention that I expect Squire Harkaway to join us this morning, and you must prepare for my departure to Oak Hall immediately.

Cool. Leave town in the middle of the season, Sir Harcourt? So unprecedented a proceeding!

Sir H. It is! I confess it; there is but one power could effect such a miracle—that is divinity.

Cool. How?

Sir H. In female form, of course. Cool, I am about to present society with a second Lady Courtley; young—blushing eighteen; lovely! I have her portrait; rich! I have her banker's account;—an heiress, and a Venus!

Cool. Lady Courtley could be none other.

Sir H. Ha! ha! Cool, your manners are above your station. Apropos, I shall find no further use for my brocade dressing-gown.

Cool. I thank you, Sir Harcourt; might I ask who the fortunate lady is?

Sir H. Certainly; Miss Grace Harkaway, the niece of my old friend, Max.

Cool. Have you never seen the lady, sir?

Sir H. Never—that is, yes—eight years ago. Having been, as you know, on the continent for the last seven years, I have had no opportunity of paying my devoirs. Our connection and bethrothal was a very extraordinary one. Her father's estates were contiguous to mine; —being a penurious, miserly, *ugly* old scoundrel, he made a market of my indiscretion, and supplied my extravagance with large sums of money on mortgages, his great desire being to unite the two properties. About seven years ago he died—leaving Grace, a girl, to the guardianship of her uncle, with this will:—if, on attaining the age of nineteen, she would consent to marry me, I should receive those deeds, and all his property, as her dowry. If she refused to comply with this condition, they should revert to my heir, presumptive or apparent. She consents.

Cool. Who would not?

Sir H. I consent to receive her £15,000. a year. (*crosses to* L.)

Cool. Who would not?

Sir H. So prepare, Cool, prepare; but where is my boy, where is Charles?

Cool. Why—oh, he is gone out, Sir Harcourt; yes, gone out to take a walk.

Sir H. Poor child! A perfect child in heart—a sober, placid mind— the simplicity and verdure of boyhood, kept fresh and unsullied by any contact with society. Tell me, Cool, at what time was he in bed last night?

Cool. Half-past nine, Sir Harcourt.

Sir H. Half-past nine! Beautiful! What an original idea! Reposing in cherub slumbers, while all around him teems with drinking and debauchery! Primitive sweetness of nature! no pilot-coated, bear-skinned* brawling!

Cool. Oh, Sir Harcourt!

Sir H. No cigar-smoking——

Cool. Faints at the smell of one.

Sir H. No brandy and water bibbing——

Cool. Doesn't know the taste of anything stronger than barley-water.

Sir H. No night parading——

Cool. Never heard the clock strike twelve, except at noon.

Sir H. In fact, he is my son, and became a gentleman by right of paternity—he inherited my manners.

Enter MARTIN, L.

Mar. Mr. Harkaway.

Enter MAX HARKAWAY, L.

Max. Squire Harkaway, fellow, or Max Harkaway, another time.
[MARTIN *bows and exit.*

---

* The peculiar style of costume worn, alike by swells, snobs, and frequenters of " Evans's " in 1841.

Ah! ha! Sir Harcourt, I'm devilish glad to see you! Gi' me your fist—dang it, but I'm glad to see you! Let me see: six—seven years or more, since we have met. How quickly they have flown!

SIR H. (*throwing off his studied manner*). Max, Max! give me your hand, old boy. (*aside*) Ah! he *is* glad to see me; there is no fawning pretence about that squeeze. Cool, you may retire. [*Exit* COOL, R. C.

MAX. Why, you are looking quite rosy.

SIR H. Ah, ah! rosy! Am I too florid?

MAX. Not a bit; not a bit.

SIR H. I thought so. (*aside*) Cool said I had put too much on.

MAX. How comes it, Courtley, you manage to retain your youth? See, I'm as gray as an old badger, or a wild rabbit; while you are—are as black as a young rook. I say, whose head grew your hair, eh?

SIR H. Permit me to remark, that all the beauties of my person are of home manufacture. Why should you be surprised at my youth? I have scarcely thrown off the giddiness of a very boy—elasticity of limb—buoyancy of soul! Remark this position. (*throws himself into an attitude*) I held that attitude for ten minutes at Lady Acid's last *reunion*, at the express desire of one of our first sculptors, while he was making a sketch of me for the Apollo.

MAX (*aside*). Making a butt of thee for their gibes.

SIR H. Lady Sarah Sarcasm started up, and, pointing to my face, ejaculated, "Good gracious! does not Sir Harcourt remind you of the countenance of Ajax, in the Pompeian portrait?"

MAX. Ajax!—humbug!

SIR H. You are complimentary.

MAX. I am a plain man, and always speak my mind. What's in a face or figure? Does a Grecian nose entail a good temper? Does a waspish waist indicate a good heart? Or, do oily perfumed locks necessarily thatch a well-furnished brain?

SIR H. It's an undeniable fact, *plain* people always praise the beauties of the *mind*.

MAX. Excuse the insinuation; I had thought the first Lady Courtley had surfeited you with beauty.

SIR H. No; she lived fourteen months with me, and then eloped with an intimate friend. Etiquette compelled me to challenge the seducer; so I received satisfaction—and a bullet in my shoulder at the same time. However, I had the consolation of knowing that he was the handsomest man of the age. She did not insult me by running away with a damned ill-looking scoundrel.

MAX. That, certainly, was flattering.

SIR H. I felt so, as I pocketed the ten thousand pounds damages

MAX. That must have been a great balm to your sore honor.

SIR H. It was—Max, my honor would have died without it; for on that year the wrong horse won the Derby—by some mistake. It was one of the luckiest chances—a thing that does not happen twice in a man's life—the opportunity of getting rid of his wife and his debts at the same time.

MAX. Tell the truth, Courtley—Did you not feel a little frayed in your delicacy—your honor, now? Eh?

SIR H. Not a whit. Why should I? I married *money*, and I received it—virgin gold! My delicacy and honor had nothing to do with it. The world pities the bereaved husband, when it should congratulate. No; the affair made a sensation, and I was the object. Besides, it is vulgar to make a parade of one's feelings, however acute they may be; impenetrability of countenance is the sure sign of your highly-bred man of fashion.

Max. So a man must, therefore, lose his wife and his money with a smile—in fact, everything he possesses but his temper.

Sir H. Exactly; and greet ruin with *vive la bagatelle!* For example: your modish beauty never discomposes the shape of her features with convulsive laughter. A smile rewards the *bon mot*, and also shows the whiteness of her teeth. She never weeps impromptu—tears might destroy the economy of her cheek. Scenes are vulgar, hysterics obsolete; she exhibits a calm, placid, impenetrable lake, whose surface is reflection, but of unfathomable depth—a statue, whose life is hypothetical, and not a *prima facie* fact.

Max Well, give me the girl that will fly at your eyes in an argument, and stick to her point like a fox to his own tail.

Sir H. But etiquette, Max! remember etiquette!

Max. Damn etiquette! I have seen a man who thought it sacrilege to eat fish with a knife. that would not scruple to rise up and rob his brother of his birth-right in a gambling-house. Your thorough-bred, well-blooded heart will seldom kick over the traces of good feeling. That's my opinion, and I don't care who knows it.

Sir H. Pardon me—etiquette is the pulse of society, by regulating which the body politic is retained in health. I consider myself one of the faculty in the art.

Max. Well, well; you are a living libel upon common sense, for you are old enough to know better.

Sir H. Old enough! What do you mean? Old! I still retain all my little juvenile indiscretions, which your niece's beauties must teach me to discard. I have not sown my wild oats yet.

Max. Time you did, at sixty-three.

Sir H. Sixty-three! Good Heavens!—forty, 'pon my life! forty, next March.

Max. Why, you are older than I am.

Sir H. Oh! you are old enough to be my father.

Max. Well, if I am, I am; that's etiquette, I suppose. Poor Grace! how often have I pitied her fate! That a young and beautiful creature should be driven into wretched splendor, or miserable poverty!

Sir H. Wretched! wherefore? Lady Courtley wretched! Impossible!

Max. Will she not be compelled to marry you, whether she likes you or not?—a choice between you and poverty. (*aside*) And hang me if it isn't a tie! But why do you not introduce your son Charles to me? I have not seen him since he was a child. You would never permit him to accept any of my invitations to spend his vacation at Oak Hall—of course, we shall have the pleasure of his company now.

Sir H. He is not fit to enter society yet. He is a studious, sober boy.

Max. Boy! Why, he's five-and-twenty.

Sir H. Good gracious! Max—you will permit me to know my own son's age—he is not twenty.

Max. I'm dumb.

Sir H. You will excuse me while I indulge in the process of dressing. Cool!

Enter Cool, r.

Prepare my toilet.   [*Exit* Cool, l.
That is a ceremony which, with me, supersedes all others. I consider it a duty which every gentleman owes to society, to render himself as agreeable an object as possible; and the least compliment a mortal can pay to nature, when she honors him by bestowing extra care in the

manufacture of his person, is to display her taste to the best possible advantage ; and so, *au revoir*.   [*Exit*, L. C.

Max. That's a good son.—he has his faults, and who has not ? Forty years of age! Oh, monstrous !—but he does look uncommonly young for sixty, spite of his foreign locks and complexion.

Enter DAZZLE, R.

Daz. Who's my friend with the stick and gaiters, I wonder—one of the family—the governor, may be ?

Max. Who's this ? Oh, Charles—is that you my boy ? How are you ? (*aside*) This is the *boy*.

Daz. He knows me—he is too respectable for a bailiff. (*aloud*) How are you ?

Max. Your father has just left me.

Daz. (*aside*) The devil he has ! He has been dead these ten years. Oh ! I see, he thinks I'm young Courtley. (*aloud*) The honor you would confer upon me, I must unwillingly disclaim—I am not Mr. Courtley.

Max. I beg pardon—a friend, I suppose ?

Daz. Oh, a most intimate friend—a friend of years—distantly related to the family—one of my ancestors married one of his. (*aside*) Adam and Eve.

Max. Are you on a visit here ?

Daz. Yes ; oh! yes. (*aside*) Rather a short one, I'm afraid.

Max (*aside*). This appears a dashing kind of fellow—as he is a friend of Sir Harcourt's, I'll invite him to the wedding. (*aloud*) Sir, if you are not otherwise engaged, I shall feel honored by your company at my house, Oak Hall, Gloucestershire.

Daz. Your name is——

Max. Harkaway—Max Harkaway.

Daz. Harkaway—let me see—I ought to be related to the Harkaways, somehow.

Max. A wedding is about to come off—will you take a part on the occasion ?

Daz. With pleasure ! any part but that of the husband.

Max. Have you any previous engagement ?

Daz. I was thinking—eh ? why, let me see. (*aside*) Promised to meet my tailor and his account to-morrow ; however, I'll postpone that. (*aloud*) Have you good shooting ?

Max. Shooting ! Why, there's no shooting at this time of the year.

Daz Oh ! I'm in no hurry—I can wait till the season, of course. I was only speaking precautionally—you have good shooting ?

Max. The best in the country.

Daz. Make yourself comfortable !—Say no more—I'm your man— wait till you see how I'll murder your preserves.

Max. Do you hunt ?

Daz. Pardon me—but will you repeat that ? (*aside*) Delicious and expensive idea !

Max. You ride ?

Daz. Anything ! Everything ! From a blood to a broomstick. Only catch me a flash of lightning, and let me get on the back of it, and dam'me if I wouldn't astonish the elements.

Max. Ha ! ha !

Daz. I'd put a girdle round about the earth in very considerably less than forty minutes.

Max. Ah ! ha ! We'll show old Fiddlestrings how to spend the day. He imagines that Nature, at the earnest request of Fashion, made summer days long for him to saunter in the Park, and winter nights that he might have good time to get cleared out at hazard or at whist. Give me the yelping of a pack of hounds before the shuffling of a pack of cards. What state can match the chase in full cry, each vieing with his fellows which shall be most happy? A thousand deaths fly by unheeded in that one hour's life of ecstacy. Time is outrun, and Nature seems to grudge our bliss by making the day so short.

Daz. No, for there rises up the idol of my great adoration.

Max. Who's that?

Daz. The bottle—that lends a lustre to the soul!—When the world puts on its night-cap, and extinguishes the sun—then comes the bottle! Oh, mighty wine! don't ask me to apostrophize. Wine and love are the only two indescribable things in nature; but I prefer the wine, because its consequences are not entailed, and are more easily got rid of.

Max. How so!

D\z. Love ends in matrimony, wine in soda water.

Maz. Well, I can promise you as fine a bottle as ever was cracked.

Daz. Never mind the bottle, give me the wine. Say no more; but, when I arrive, just shake one of my hands, and put the key of the cellar into the other, and if I don't make myself intimately acquainted with its internal organization—well, I say nothing—time will show.

Max. I foresee some happy days.

Daz. And I some glorious nights.

Max. It mustn't be a flying visit.

Daz. I despise the word—I'll stop a month with you.

Max. Or a year or two.

Daz I'll live and die with you!

Max. Ha! ha! Remember Max Harkaway, Oak Hall, Gloucestershire.

Daz. I'll remember—fare ye well. (Max *is going*) ⁀ say, holloa!—Tallyho-o-o-o!

Max. Yoicks!—Tallyhoa-o-o-o!	[*Exit*, L.

Daz. There I am—quartered for a couple of years, at the least. The old boy wants somebody to ride his horses, shoot his game, and keep a restraint on the morals of the parish: I'm eligible. What a lucky accident to meet Young Courtley last night! Who could have thought it? Yesterday, I could not make certain of a dinner, except at my own proper peril; to-day I would flirt with a banquet.

Enter Young Courtley, R.

Young C. What infernal row was that? Why, (*seeing* Dazzle) are you here still?

Daz. Yes. Ain't you delighted? I'll ring, and send the servant for my luggage.

' Young C. The devil you will! Why, you don't mean to say you seriously intend to take up a permanent residence here? (*rings the bell.*)

Daz. Now, that's a most inhospitable insinuation.

Young C. Might I ask your name?

Daz. With a deal of pleasure—Richard Dazzle, late of the Unattached Volunteers, vulgarly entitled the Dirty Buffs.

Enter Martin, R.

Young C. Then, Mr. Richard Dazzle, I have the honor of wishing you a very good morning. Martin, show this gentleman the door.

Daz. If he does, I'll kick Martin out of it. No offence.

                              [*Exit* Martin, l.

Now, sir, permit me to place a dioramic view of your conduct before you. After bringing you safely home this morning—after indulgently waiting, whenever you took a passing fancy to a knocker or bell-pull—after conducting a retreat that would have reflected honor on Napoleon—you would kick me into the street, like a mangy cur; and that's what you call gratitude. Now, to show you how superior I am to petty malice, I give you an unlimited invitation to my house—my country house—to remain as long as you please.

Young C. Your house!

Daz. Oak Hall, Gloucestershire—fine old place!—for further particulars see road book—that is, it *nominally* belongs to my old friend and relation, Max Harkaway ; but I'm privileged. Capital old fellow—say, shall we be honored ?

Young C. Sir, permit me to hesitate a moment. (*aside*) Let me see : I go back to college to-morrow, so I shall not be missing ; tradesmen begin to dun——

Enter Cool, r.

I hear thunder ; here is shelter ready for me.

Cool. Oh, Mr. Charles, Mr. Solomon Isaacs is in the hall, and swears he will remain till he has arrested you!

Young C. Does he !—sorry he is so obstinate—take him my compliments, and I will bet him five to one he will not.

Daz. Double or quits, with my kind regards.

Cool. But, sir, he has discovered the house in Curzon street ; he says he is aware the furniture at least belongs to you, and he will put a man in immediately.

Young C. That's awkward—what's to be done ?

Daz. Ask him whether he couldn't make it a woman.

Young C. I must trust that to fate.

Daz. I will give you my acceptance, if it will be of any use to you—it is of none to me.

Young C. No, sir ; but in reply to your most generous and kind invitation, if you be in earnest, I shall feel delighted to accept it.

Daz. Certainly.

Young C. Then off we go—through the stables—down the Mews, and so slip through my friend's fingers.

Daz. But, stay, you must do the polite ; say farewell to him before you part. Damn it, don't cut him !

Young C. You jest!

Daz. Here, lend me a card. (Courtley *gives him one*) Now, then, (*writes*) "Our respects to Mr. Isaacs—sorry to have been prevented from seeing him." Ha! ha!

Young C. Ha! ha!

Daz. We'll send him up some game.

Young C. (*to* Cool). Don't let my father see him.

                       [*Exeunt* Young Courtley *and* Dazzle, r.

Cool. What's this ? "Mr. Charles Courtley, P. P. C , returns thanks for obliging inquiries."   [*Exit*, l.

CURTAIN.

ACT II.

SCENE.—*The lawn before Oak Hall, a fine Elizabethan mansion; a drawing-room is seen through large French windows at the back. Statues, urns and garden chairs about the stage.*

Enter PERT *and* JAMES, L.

PERT. James, Miss Grace desires me to request that you will watch at the avenue and let her know when the squire's carriage's seen on the London road.

JAMES. I will go to the lodge.　　　　　[*Exit*, L.

PERT. How I do long to see what kind of a man Sir Harcourt Courtley is! They say he is sixty; so he must be old, and consequently ugly. If I was Miss Grace, I would rather give up all my fortune and marry the man I liked, than go to church with a stuffed eel-skin. But taste is everything—she doesn't seem to care whether he is sixty or sixteen; jokes at love; prepares for matrimony as she would for dinner; says it is a necessary evil, and what can't be cured must be endured. Now, I say this is against all nature; and she is either no woman, or a deeper one than I am, if she prefers an old man to a young one. Here she comes! looking as cheerfully as if she was going to marry Mr. Jenks! My Mr. Jenks! whom nobody wont lead to the halter till I have that honor.

Enter GRACE, *from drawing-room*, L.

GRACE. Well, Pert! any signs of the squire yet?

PERT. No, Miss Grace; but James has gone to watch the road.

GRACE. In my uncle's letter he mentions a Mr. Dazzle, whom he has invited; so you must prepare a room for him. He is some friend of my husband that is to be, and my uncle seems to have taken an extra-ordinary predilection for him. Apropos! I must not forget to have a bouquet for the dear old man when he arrives.

PERT. The dear old man! Do you mean Sir Harcourt?

GRACE. La, no! my uncle of course. (*plucking flowers*) What do I care for Sir Harcourt Courtley? (*crosses* R.)

PERT. Isn't it odd, Miss, you have never seen your intended, though it has been so long since you were betrothed?

GRACE. Not at all; marriage matters are conducted now-a-days in a most mercantile manner; consequently, a previous acquaintance is by no means indispensable. Besides, my prescribed husband has been upon the continent for the benefit of his—property! They say a southern climate is a great restorer of consumptive estates.

PERT. Well, Miss, for my own part, I should like to have a good look at my bargain before I paid for it; 'specially when one's life is the price of the article. But why, ma'am, do you consent to marry in this blind-man's-buff sort of manner? What would you think if he were not quite so old?

GRACE. I should think he was a little younger.

PERT. I should like him all the better.

GRACE. That wouldn't I. A young husband might expect affection and nonsense, which 'twould be deceit in me to render; nor would he permit me to remain with my uncle. Sir Harcourt takes me with the incumbrances on his estate, and I shall beg to be left among the rest of the live stock.

PERT. Ah, Miss! but some day you might chance to stumble over *the* man—what could you do then ?

GRACE. Do! beg *the* man's pardon, and request *the* man to pick me up again.

PERT. Ah ! you were never in love, Miss.

GRACE. I never was, nor will be, till I am tired of myself and common sense. Love is a pleasant scape-goat for a little epidemic madness. I must have been inoculated in my infancy, for the infection passes over poor me in contempt.

Enter JAMES, L.

JAMES. Two gentlemen, Miss Grace, have just alighted.

GRACE. Very well, James.   [*Exit* JAMES, L.
Love is pictured as a boy ; in another century they will be wiser, and paint him as a fool, with cap and bells, without a thought above the jingling of his own folly. Now, Pert, remember this as a maxim—A woman is always in love with one of two things.

PERT. What are they, Miss ?

GRACE. A man, or herself—and I know which is the most profitable.
                                        [*Exit*, L.

PERT. I wonder what my Jenks would say, if I was to ask him. La ! here comes Mr. Meddle, his rival, contemporary solicitor, as he calls him—a nasty, prying, ugly wretch—what brings him here ? He comes puffed with some news. (*retires up* R.)

Enter MEDDLE, *with newspaper*, L.

MED. I have secured the only newspaper in the village—my character, as an attorney-at-law, depended on the monopoly of its information. I took it up by chance, when this paragraph met my astonished view: (*reads*) " We understand that the contract of marriage so long in abeyance on account of the lady's minority, is about to be celebrated at Oak Hall, Gloucestershire, the well-known and magnificent mansion of Maximilian Harkaway, Esq., between Sir Harcourt Courtley, baronet, of fashionable celebrity, and Miss Grace Harkaway, niece to the said Mr. Harkaway. The preparations are proceeding in the good old English style." Is it possible ! I seldom swear, except in a witness box, but, damme, had it been known in the village, my reputation would have been lost ; my voice in the parlor of the Red Lion mute, and Jenks, a fellow who calls himself a lawyer, without more capability than a broomstick, and as much impudence as a young barrister after getting a verdict by mistake ; why, he would actually have taken the Reverend Mr. Spout by the button, which is now my sole privilege. (*sees* PERT) Ah ! here is Mrs. Pert ; couldn't have hit upon a better person. I'll cross-examine her—lady's maid to Miss Grace—confidential purloiner of second-hand silk—a *nisi prius* of her mistress—Ah ! sits on the woolsack in the pantry, and dictates the laws of kitchen etiquette. (PERT *comes forward*) Ah ! Mrs. Pert, good-morning ; permit me to say—and my word as a legal character is not unduly considered—I venture to affirm, that you look a—quite like the—a——

PERT. Law ! Mr. Meddle.

MED. Exactly like the law.

PERT. Ha! indeed ; complimentary, I confess ; like the law ; tedious, prosy, made up of musty paper. You sha'n't have a long suit of me. Good-morning. (*going.*)

MED. Stay, Mrs. Pert; don't calumniate my calling, or disseminate vulgar prejudices.

PERT. Vulgar! you talk of vulgarity to me! you, whose sole employment is to sneak about like a pig, snouting out the dust-hole of society, and feeding upon the bad ends of vice! you, who live upon the world's iniquity; you miserable specimen of a bad six-and-eightpence!

MED. But, Mrs. Pert—

PERT. Don't but me, sir; I won't be butted by any such low fellow.

MED. This is slander; an action will lie.

PERT. Let it lie; lying is your trade. I'll tell you what, Mr. Meddle; if I had my will, I would soon put a check to your prying propensities. I'd treat you as the farmers do inquisitive hogs.

MED. How?

PERT. I would ring your nose.   [Exit, L.

MED. Not much information elicited from that witness. Jenks is at the bottom of this. I have very little hesitation in saying, Jenks is a libellous rascal; I heard reports that he was undermining my character here, through Mrs. Pert. Now I'm certain of it. Assault is expensive; but I certainly will put by a small weekly stipendium, until I can afford to kick Jenks.

DAZ. (outside). Come along; this way!

MED. Ah! whom have we here? Visitors; I'll address them.

Enter DAZZLE, L.

DAZ. Who's this, I wonder; one of the family? I must know him. (to MEDDLE) Ah! how are ye?

MED. Quite well. Just arrived?—ah!—um! Might I request the honor of knowing whom I address?

DAZ Richard Dazzle, Esquire; and you——

MED. Mark Meddle, attorney-at-law.

Enter YOUNG COURTLEY, L.

DAZ. What detained you?

YOUNG C. My dear fellow, I have just seen such a woman——

DAZ. (aside). Hush! (aloud) Permit me to introduce you to my very old friend, Meddle. He's a capital fellow; know him.

MED. I feel honored. Who is your friend?

DAZ. Oh, he? What, my friend? Oh! Augustus Hamilton.

YOUNG C How d'ye do? (looking off) There she is again!

MED (looking off). Why, that is Miss Grace.

DAZ. Of course, Grace.

YOUNG C. I'll go and introduce myself. (DAZZLE stops him.)

DAZ. (aside). What are you about? would you insult my old friend Puddle by running away? (aloud) I say, Puddle, just show my friend the lions, while I say how d'ye do to my young friend Grace. (aside) Cultivate his acquaintance.

[Exit, L. YOUNG COURTLEY looks after him.

MED. Mr. Hamilton, might I take the liberty?

YOUNG C. (looking off). Confound the fellow!

MED. Sir, what did you remark?

YOUNG C. She's gone! Oh, are you here still, Mr. Thingomerry Puddle?

MED. Meddle, sir, Meddle, in the list of attorneys.

YOUNG C. Well, Muddle, or Puddle, or whoever you are, you are a bore.

MED. (*aside*). How excessively odd! Mrs. Pert said I was a pig; now I'm a boar! I wonder what they'll make of me next.

YOUNG C. Mr. Thingamy, will you take a word of advice?

MED. Feel honored.

YOUNG C. Get out.

MED. Do you mean to—I don't understand.

YOUNG C. Delighted to quicken your apprehension. You are an ass, Puddle.

MED. Ha! ha! another quadruped! Yes; beautiful. (*aside*) I wish he'd call me something libellous; but that would be too much to expect. (*aloud*) Anything else?

YOUNG C. Some miserable pettifogging scoundrel!

MED. Good! ha! ha!

YOUNG C. What do you mean by laughing at me?

MED. Ha! ha! ha! excellent! delicious!

YOUNG C. Mr. ——, are you ambitious of a kicking?

MED. Very, very—Go on—kick—go on.

YOUNG C. (*looking off*). Here she comes! I'll speak to her.

MED. But, sir—sir——

YOUNG C. Oh, go to the devil!   [*Runs off*, L.

MED. There, there's a chance lost—gone! I have no hesitation in saying that, in another minute, I should have been kicked; literally kicked—a legal luxury. Costs, damages, and actions rose up like sky-rockets in my aspiring soul, with golden tails reaching to the infinity of my hopes. (*looking*) They are coming this way; Mr. Hamilton in close conversation with Lady Courtley that is to be. Crim. Con. Courtley versus Hamilton—damage, problematical—Meddle, chief witness for plaintiff—guinea a-day—professional man! I'll take down their conversation verbatim.   [*Retires behind a bush*, R.

Enter GRACE, *followed by* YOUNG COURTLEY, L.

GRACE. Perhaps you would follow you friend into the dining-room; refreshment, after your long journey, must be requisite.

YOUNG C. Pardon me, madam; but the lovely garden and the loveliness before me, is better refreshment than I could procure in any dining-room.

GRACE. Ha! Your company and compliments arrive together.

YOUNG C. I trust that passing remark will not spoil so welcome an introduction as this by offending you.

GRACE. I am not certain that anything you could say would offend me.

YOUNG C. I never meant——

GRACE. I thought not. In turn, pardon me, when I request you will commence your visit with this piece of information:—I consider compliments impertinent, and sweetmeat language fulsome.

YOUNG C. I would condemn my tongue to a Pythagorean silence, if I thought it could attempt to flatter.

GRACE. It strikes me, sir, that you are a stray bee from the hive of fashion; if so, reserve your honey for its proper cell. A truce to compliments.—You have just arrived *from town*, I apprehend.

YOUNG C. This moment I left mighty London, under the fever of a full season, groaning with the noisy pulse of wealth and the giddy whirling brain of fashion. Enchanting, busy London! how have I prevailed on myself to desert you! Next week the new ballet comes out —the week after comes Ascot. Oh!

GRACE. How agonizing must be the reflection!

Young C. Torture! Can you inform me how you manage to avoid suicide here? If there was but an opera, even, within twenty miles! We couldn't get up a rustic ballet among the village girls? No!—ah!

Grace. I am afraid you would find that difficult. How I contrive to support life I don't know—it is wonderful—but I have not precisely contemplated suicide yet, nor do I miss the opera.

Young C. How can you manage to kill time?

Grace. I can't. Men talk of killing time, while time quietly kills them. I have many employments—this week I devote to study and various amusements—next week to being married—the following week to repentance, perhaps.

Young C. Married!

Grace. You seem surprised; I believe it is of frequent occurrence in the metropolis—is it not?

Young C. Might I ask to whom?

Grace. A gentleman who has been strongly recommended to me for the situation of husband.

Young C. What an extraordinary match! Would you not consider it advisable to see him, previous to incurring the consequences of such an act?

Grace. You must be aware that fashion says otherwise. The gentleman swears eternal devotion to the lady's fortune, and the lady swears she will outlive him still. My lord's horses and my lady's diamonds shine through a few seasons, until a seat in Parliament, or the continent stares them in the face; then, when thrown upon each other for resources of comfort, they begin to quarrel about the original conditions of the sale.

Young C. Sale! No! that would be degrading civilization into Turkish barbarity.

Grace. Worse, sir, a great deal worse; for there at least they do not attempt concealment of the barter; but here, every London ball-room is a marriage mart—young ladies are trotted out, while the mother, father, or chaperone plays auctioneer, and knocks them down to the highest bidder—young men are ticketed up with fortunes on their backs—and Love, turned into a dapper shopman, descants on the excellent qualities of the material.

Young C. Oh! that such a custom could have ever emanated from the healthy soil of an English heart!

Grace. No; it never did—like most of our literary dandyisms and dandy literature, it was borrowed from the French.

Young C. You seem to laugh at love.

Grace. Love! why, the very word is a breathing satire upon man's reason—a mania, indigenous to humanity—nature's jester, who plays off tricks upon the world, and trips up common sense. When I'm in love, I'll write an almanac, for the very lack of wit—prognosticate the sighing season—when to beware of tears—about this time expect matrimony to be prevalent! Ha! ha! Why should I lay out my life in love's bonds upon the bare security of a man's word?

Enter JAMES, L.

JAMES. The squire, madam, has just arrived, and another gentleman with him.

Grace (*aside*). My intended, I suppose. [*Exit* JAMES, L.

Young C. I perceive you are one of the railers against what is termed the follies of high life.

GRACE. No, not particularly; I deprecate all folly. By what prerogative can the west-end mint issue absurdity, which, if coined in the east, would be voted vulgar?

YOUNG C. By a sovereign right—because it has Fashion's head upon its side, and that stamps it current.

GRACE. Poor Fashion, for how many sins hast thou to answer! The gambler pawns his birth-right for fashion—the *roue* steals his friend's wife for fashion—each abandons himself to the storm of impulse, calling it the breeze of fashion.

YOUNG C. Is this idol of the world so radically vicious?

GRACE. No; the root is well enough, as the body was, until it had outgrown its native soil; but now, like a mighty giant lying over Europe, it pillows its head in Italy, its heart in France, leaving the heels alone its sole support for England.

YOUNG C. Pardon me, madam, you wrong yourself to rail against your own inheritance—the kingdom to which loveliness and wit attest your title.

GRACE. A mighty realm, forsooth—with milliners for ministers, a cabinet of coxcombs, envy for my homage, ruin for my revenue—my right of rule depending on the shape of a bonnet or the set of a pelisse, with the next grand noodle as my heir-apparent. Mr. Hamilton, when I am crowned, I shall feel happy to abdicate in your favor.

[*Curtesy and exit*, L.

YOUNG C. What did she mean by that? Damme if I can understand her—she is evidently not used to society. Ha!—takes every word I say for infallible truth—requires the solution of a compliment, as if it were a problem in Euclid. She said she was about to marry, but I rather imagine she was in jest. 'Pon my life, I feel very queer at the contemplation of such an idea—I'll follow her. (MEDDLE *comes down*) Oh! perhaps this booby can inform me something about her. (MEDDLE *makes signs at him*) What the devil is he at?

MED. It won't do—no—ah! um—it's not to be done.

YOUNG C. What do you mean?

MED. (*points after* GRACE). Counsel retained—cause to come off.

YOUNG C. Cause to come off!

MED. Miss Grace is about to be married.

YOUNG C. Is it possible?

MED. Certainly. If I have the drawing out of the deeds——

YOUNG C. To whom?

MED. Ha! hem! Oh, yes! I dare say—information being scarce in the market, I hope to make mine valuable.

YOUNG C. Married! married!

MED. Now I shall have another chance.

YOUNG C. I'll run and ascertain the truth of this from Dazzle.

[*Exit*, L.

MED. It's of no use; he either dare not kick me, or he can't afford it—in either case, he is beneath my notice. Ah! who comes here?—can it be Sir Harcourt Courtley himself? It can be no other.

Enter COOL, L.

Sir, I have the honor to bid you welcome to Oak Hall and the village of Oldborough,

COOL (*aside*). Excessively polite. (*aloud*) Sir, thank you

MED. The township contains two thousand inhabitants.

COOL. Does it? I am delighted to hear it.

MED. (*aside*). I can charge him for that—ahem—six and eightpence is not much—but it is a beginning. (*aloud*) If you will permit me, I can inform you of the different commodities for which it is famous.

Cool. Much obliged—but here comes Sir Harcourt Courtley, my master, and Mr. Harkaway—any other time I shall feel delighted.

Med. Oh! (*aside*) Mistook the man for the master. (*retires up* R.)

Enter Max *and* Sir Harcourt, L.

Max. Here we are at last. Now give ye welcome to Oak Hall, Sir Harcourt, heartily!

Sir H. (*languidly*). Cool, assist me. (Cool *takes off his cloak and gloves ; gives him white gloves and handkerchief.*)

Max. Why, you require unpacking as carefully as my best bin of port. Well, now you are decanted, tell me what did you think of my park as we came along?

Sir H. That it would never come to an end. You said it was only a stone's throw from your infernal lodge to the house; why, it's ten miles, at least.

Max. I'll do it in ten minutes any day.

Sir H. Yes, in a steam carriage. Cool, perfume my handkerchief.

Max. Don't do it. Don't! perfume in the country! why, it's high treason in the very face of Nature; 'tis introducing the robbed to the robber. Here are the sweets from which your fulsome essences are pilfered, and labelled with their names; don't insult them, too. (Meddle *comes down, c.*)

Sir H. (*to* Meddle). Oh! cull me a bouquet, my man!

Max (*turning*). Ah, Meddle! how are you? This is Lawyer Meddle.

Sir H. Oh! I took him for one of your people.

Med. Ah! naturally—um—Sir Harcourt Courtley, I have the honor to congratulate—happy occasion approaches. Ahem! I have no hesitation in saying this *very* happy occasion approaches.

Sir H. Cool, is the conversation addressed towards me?

Cool. I believe so, Sir Harcourt.

Med. Oh, certainly! I was complimenting you.

Sir H. Sir, you are very good; the honor is undeserved; but I am only in the habit of receiving compliments from the fair sex. Men's admiration is so damnably insipid.

Med. I had hoped to make a unit on that occasion.

Sir H. Yes, and you hoped to put an infernal number of cyphers after your unit on that and any other occasion.

Med. Ha! ha! very good. Why, I did hope to have the honor of drawing out the deeds; for, whatever Jenks may say to the contrary, I have no hesitation in saying——

Sir H. (*putting him aside. To* Max). If the future Lady Courtley be visible at so unfashionable an hour as this, I shall beg to be introduced.

Max. Visible! Ever since six this morning, I'll warrant ye. Two to one she is at dinner.

Sir H. Dinner! Is it possible? Lady Courtley dine at half-past one P. M.?

Med. I rather prefer that hour to peck a little my——

Sir H. Dear me! who was addressing you?

Med. Oh! I beg pardon.

Max. Here, James! (*calling.*)

Enter James, L.

Tell Miss Grace to come here directly.   [*Exit* JAMES, L.

Now prepare, Courtley, for, though I say it, she is—with the exception of my bay mare, Kitty—the handsomest thing in the country. Considering she is a biped, she is a wonder!. Full of blood, sound wind and limb, plenty of bone, sweet coat, in fine condition, with a thorough-bred step, as dainty as a pet greyhound.

SIR H. Damme, don't compare her to a horse!

MAX. Well, I wouldn't, but she's almost as fine a creature—close similarities.

MED. Oh, very fine creature! Close similarity, amounting to identity.

SIR H. Good gracious, sir! What can a lawyer know about women?

MED. Everything. The consistorial court is a fine study of the character, and I have no hesitation in saying that I have examined more women than Jenks, or——

SIR H. Oh, d—n Jenks!

MED. Sir, thank you. D—n him again, sir, d—n him again!

Enter GRACE, L.

GRACE. My dear uncle!

MAX. Ah, Grace, you little jade, come here.

SIR H. (*eyeing her through his glass*). Oh, dear! she is a rural Venus! I'm astonished and delighted.

MAX. Won't you kiss your old uncle? (*kisses her.*)

SIR H. (*draws an agonizing face*). Oh!—ah—um!—*N'importe!*— my privilege in embryo—hem! It's very tantalizing, though.

MAX. You are not glad to see me, you are not. (*kissing her again.*)

SIR H. Oh; no, no! (*aside*) that is too much. I shall do something horrible presently if this goes on. (*aloud*) I should be sorry to curtail any little ebullition of affection; but—ahem! May I be permitted?

MAX. Of course you may. There, Grace, is Sir Harcourt, your husband that will be. Go to him, girl.

SIR H. Permit me to do homage to the charms, the presence of which have placed me in sight of Paradise.

[SIR HARCOURT *and* GRACE *retire.*

Enter DAZZLE, L.

DAZ. Ah! old fellow, how are you?

MAX. I'm glad to see you. Are you comfortably quartered yet, eh?

DAZ. Splendidly quartered! What a place you've got here! Here, Hamilton.

Enter YOUNG COURTLEY.

Permit me to introduce my friend, Augustus Hamilton. Capital fellow! drinks like a sieve, and rides like a thunder-storm.

MAX. Sir, I'm devilish glad to see you. Here, Sir Harcourt, permit me to introduce to you——

YOUNG C. The devil!

DAZ. (*aside*). What's the matter?

YOUNG C. (*aside*). Why, that is my governor, by Jupiter!

DAZ (*aside*). What, old Whiskers! you don't say that?

YOUNG C. (*aside*). It is; what's to be done now?

MAX Mr. Hamilton, Sir Harcourt Courtley—Sir Harcourt Courtley, Mr. Hamilton.

SIR H. Hamilton? Good gracious! God bless me! Why, Charles, is it possible?—why, Max, that's my son!

YOUNG C. (*aside*). What shall I do?

MAX. Your son?

GRACE. Your son, Sir Harcourt! have you a son as old as that gentleman!

SIR H. No—that is—a yes,—not by twenty years—a—Charles, why don't you answer me, sir?

YOUNG C. (*aside to* DAZZLE). What shall I say?

DAZ. (*aside*). Deny your identity.

YOUNG C. (*aside*). Capital! (*aloud*) What's the matter, sir?

SIR H. How came you down here, sir?

YOUNG C. By one of Newman's best fours—in twelve hours and a quarter.

SIR H. Isn't your name Charles Courtley?

YOUNG C. Not to my knowledge.

SIR H. Do you mean to say that you are usually called Augustus Hamilton?

YOUNG C. Lamentable fact—and quite correct.

SIR H. Cool, is that my son?

COOL. No, sir—it is not Mr. Charles—but it is very like him.

MAX. I cannot understand all this. (*goes up.*)

GRACE. (*aside*). I think I can.

DAZ. (*aside to* YOUNG C.). Give him a touch of the indignant.

YOUNG C. Allow me to say, Sir What-d'ye-call-'em Hartly——

SIR H. Hartly, sir! Courtley, sir! Courtley!

YOUNG C. Well, Hartly, or Court-heart, or whatever your name may be, I say your conduct is—a—a—, and were it not for the presence of this lady, I should feel inclined—to—to——

SIR H. No, no, that can't be my son,—he never would address me in that way.

MAX (*coming down*). What is all this?

SIR H. Sir, your likeness to my son Charles is so astonishing, that it, for a moment—the equilibrium of my etiquette—'pon my life, I—permit me to request your pardon.

MED. Sir Harcourt, don't apologize, don't—bring an action. I'm witness.

SIR H. Some one take this man away.

Enter JAMES, L.

JAMES. Luncheon is on the table, sir.

SIR H. Miss Harkaway, I never swore before a lady in my life—except when I promised to love and cherish the late Lady Courtley, which I took care to preface with an apology,—I was compelled to the ceremony, and consequently not answerable for the language—but to that gentleman's identity I would have pledged—my hair.

GRACE (*aside*). If that security were called for, I suspect the answer would be—no effects.　　[*Exeunt* SIR HARCOURT *and* GRACE, L.

MED. (*to* MAX). I have something very particular to communicate.

MAX. Can't listen at present.　　　　　　　　　　　　[*Exit*, L.

MED. (*to* DAZZLE *and* YOUNG C.). I can afford you information, which I——

DAZ. Oh, don't bother! ⎫
YOUNG C. Go to the devil! ⎭　　　　　　　　　[*Exeunt*, L.

MED. Now, I have no hesitation in saying that is the height of ingratitude.—Oh—Mr. Cool—can you oblige me? (*presents his account.*) ⁄

Cool. Why, what is all this?

Med. Small account *versus* you—to giving information concerning the last census of the population of Oldborough and vicinity, six and eightpence.

Cool. Oh, you mean to make me pay for this, do you?

Med. Unconditionally.

Cool. Well, I have no objection—the charge is fair—but remember, I am a servant on board wages,—will you throw in a little advice gratis—if I give you the money?

Med. Ahem!—I will.

Cool. A fellow has insulted me. I want to abuse him—what terms are actionable?

Med. You may call him anything you please, providing there are no witnesses.

Cool. Oh, may I? (*looks around*) then you rascally, pettifogging scoundrel!

Med. Hallo!

Cool. You mean—dirty—disgrace to your profession.

Med. Libel—slander—

Cool. Ay, but where are your witnesses?

Med. Give me the costs—six and eightpence.

Cool. I deny that you gave me information at all.

Med. You do!

Cool. Yes, where are your witnesses?   [*Exit, L.*

Med. Ah—damme!   [*Exit, L.*

CURTAIN.

ACT III.

SCENE.—*A morning room in Oak Hall, French windows opening to the lawn.* Max *and* Sir Harcourt *seated on one side,* Dazzle *on the other ;* Grace *and* Young Courtley *playing chess at back. All dressed for dinner.*

Max. (*aside to* Sir Harcourt). What can I do?

Sir H. Get rid of them civilly.

Max. What, turn them out, after I particularly invited them to stay a month or two?

Sir H. Why, they are disreputable characters ; as for that young fellow, in whom my Lady Courtley appears so particularly absorbed—I am bewildered—I have written to town for my Charles, my boy—it certainly is the most extraordinary likeness——

Daz. Sir Harcourt, I have an idea——

Sir H. Sir, I am delighted to hear it. (*aside to* Max) That fellow is a swindler.

Max I met him at your house.

Sir H. Never saw him before in all my life.

Daz. (*crossing to* Sir Harcourt). I will bet you five to one that I can beat you three out of four games of billiards, with one hand.

Sir H. No, sir.

Daz. I don't mind giving you ten points in fifty.

Sir H. Sir, I never gamble.

Daz. You don't! Well, I'll teach you—easiest thing in life—you have every requisite—good temper.

Sir H. I have not, sir.

DAZ. A long-headed, knowing old buck.

SIR H. Sir! (*they go up, conversing with* MAX, c.)

GRACE. Really, Mr. Hamilton, you improve. A yo·· ·· ··· pays us a visit, as you half intimate, to escape inconvenient frien···—tha' is complimentary to us, his hosts.

YOUNG C. Nay, that is too severe.

GRACE. After an acquaintanceship of two days, you sit down to teach me chess and domestic economy at the same time. Might I ask where you graduated in that science—where you learned all that store of matrimonial advice which you have obliged me with? (*they come forward.*)

YOUNG C. I imbibed it, madam, from the moment I beheld you, and having studied my subject *con amore*, took my degrees from your eyes.

GRACE. Oh, I see you are a Master of Arts already.

YOUNG C. Unfortunately, no—I shall remain a bachelor—till you can assist me to that honor. (SIR HARCOURT *comes down—aside to* DAZZLE) Keep the old boy away.

DAZ. (*aside*). How do you get on?

YOUNG C. (*aside*). Splendidly!

SIR H. Is the conversation strictly confidential?—or might I join?

DAZ. (*taking his arm*). Oh, not in the least, my dear sir—we were remarking that rifle shooting was an excellent diversion during the summer months.

SIR H. (*drawing himself up*). Sir, I was add.essing——

DAZ. And I was saying what a pity it was I couldn't find any one reasonable enough to back his opinion with long odds—come out on the lawn, and pitch up your hat. and I will hold you ten to one I put a bullet into it every time, at forty paces.

SIR H. No, sir—I consider you——

MAX. Here, all of you—look, here is Lady Gay Spanker coming across the lawn at a hand gallop!

SIR H. (*running to window*). Bless me, the horse is running away!

MAX. Look how she takes that fence! there's a seat.

SIR H. Lady Gay Spanker—who may she be?

GRACE. Gay Spanker, Sir Harcourt? My cousin and dearest friend— you *must* like her.

SIR H. It will be my devoir, since it is your wish—though it will be a hard task in your presence.

GRACE. I am sure she will like you.

SIR H. Ha! ha! I flatter myself.

YOUNG C. Who, and what is she?

GRACE. Glee, glee, made a living thing—Nature, in some frolic mood, shut up a merry devil in her eye, and, spiting Art, stole Joy's brightest harmony to thrill her laugh, which peals out sorrow's knell. Her cry rings loudest in the field—the very echo loves it best, and as each hill attempts to ape her voice, Earth seems to laugh that it made a thing so glad.

MAX. Ay, the merriest minx I ever kissed. (LADY GAY *laughs without.*)

LADY GAY (*without*). Max!

MAX. Come in, you mischievous puss.

Enter JAMES, L.

JAMES. Mr. Adolphus and Lady Gay Spanker.   [*Exit.*

Enter LADY GAY, L., *fully equipped in riding habit, etc.*

LADY G. Ha! ha! Well, governor, how are ye? I have been down five times, climbing up your stairs in my long clothes. How are you, Grace, dear? (*kisses her*) There, don't fidget, Max. And there—(*kisses him*) there's one for you.

SIR H. Ahem!

LADY G. Oh, gracious, I didn't see you had visitors.

MAX. Permit me to introduce—Sir Harcourt Courtley, Lady Gay Spanker. Mr. Dazzle, Mr. Hamilton—Lady Gay Spanker.

SIR H. (*aside*). A devilish fine woman!

DAZ (*aside to* SIR HARCOURT). She's a devilish fine woman.

LADY G. You mustn't think anything of the liberties I take with my old papa here—bless him!

SIR H. Oh, no! (*aside*) I only thought I should like to be in his place.

LADY G. I am so glad you have come, Sir Harcourt. Now we shall be able to make a decent figure at the heels of a hunt.

SIR H. Does your ladyship hunt?

LADY G. Ha! I say, governor, does my ladyship hunt? I rather flatter myself that I do hunt! Why, Sir Harcourt, one might as well live without laughing as without hunting. Man was fashioned expressly to fit a horse. Are not hedges and ditches created for leaps? Of course! And I look upon foxes to be one of the most blessed dispensations of a benign Providence.

SIR H. Yes, it is all very well in the abstract; I tried it once.

LADY G. Once! Only once?

SIR H. Once, only once. And then the animal ran away with me.

LADY G. Why, you would not have him walk?

SIR H. Finding my society disagreeable, he instituted a series of kicks, with a view of removing the annoyance; but aided by the united stays of the mane and tail, I frustrated his intentions. (*all laugh*) His next resource, however, was more effectual, for he succeeded in rubbing me off against a tree.

MAX *and* LADY G. Ha! ha! ha!

DAZ. How absurd you must have looked with your legs and arms in the air. like a shipwrecked tea-table.

SIR H. Sir, I never looked absurd in my life. Ah, it may be very amusing in relation, I dare say, but very unpleasant in effect.

LADY G. I pity you, Sir Harcourt; it was criminal in your parents to neglect your education so shamefully.

SIR H. Possibly; but be assured, I shall never break my neck awkwardly from a horse, when it might be accomplished with less trouble from a bed-room window.

YOUNG C. (*aside*). My dad will be caught by this she Bucephalus-tamer.

MAX. Ah! Sir Harcourt, had you been here a month ago, you would have witnessed the most glorious run that ever swept over merry England's green cheek—a steeple-chase, sir, which I intended to win, but my horse broke down the day before. I had a chance, notwithstanding, and but for Gay here, I should have won. How I regretted my absence from it! How did my filly behave herself, Gay?

LADY G. Gloriously, Max! gloriously! There were sixty horses in the field, all mettle to the bone; the start was a picture—away we went in a cloud—pell-mell—helter-skelter—the fools first, as usual, using themselves up—we soon passed them—first your Kitty, then my Blue-

skin, and Craven's colt last. Then came the tug—Kitty skimmed the
walls—Blueskin flew over the fences—the colt neck-and-neck, and half
a mile to run—at last the colt baulked a leap and went wild. Kitty
and I had it all to ourselves—she was three lengths ahead as we
breasted the last wall, six feet, if an inch, and a ditch on the other side.
Now, for the first time, I gave Blueskin his head—ha! ha! Away he
flew like a thunderbolt—over went the filly—I over the same spot, leaving Kitty in the ditch—walked the steeple, eight miles in thirty minutes,
and scarcely turned a hair.

ALL. Bravo! Bravo!

LADY G. Do you hunt?

DAZ. Hunt! I belong to a hunting family. I was born on horseback
and cradled in a kennel! Ay, and I hope I may die with a whoo-
whoop!

MAX (to SIR HARCOURT). You must leave your town habits in the
smoke of London; here we rise with the lark.

SIR H. Haven't the remotest conception when that period is.

GRACE. The man that misses sunrise loses the sweetest part of his
existence.

SIR H. Oh, pardon me; I have seen sunrise frequently after a ball,
or from the windows of my travelling carriage, and I always considered
it disagreeable.

GRACE. I love to watch the first tear that glistens in the opening eye
of morning, the silent song the flowers breathe, the thrilling choir of
the woodland minstrels, to which the modest brook trickles applause:
these swelling out the sweetest chord of sweet creation's matins, seem
to pour some soft and merry tale into the daylight's ear, as if the wak-
ing world had dreamed a happy thing, and now smiled o'er the telling
of it.

SIR H. The effect of a rustic education! Who could ever discover
music in a damp foggy morning, except those confounded waits, who
never play in tune, and a miserable wretch who makes a point of crying coffee under my window just as I am persuading myself to sleep:
in fact, I never heard any music worth listening to, except in Italy.

LADY G. No? then you never heard a well-trained English pack in
full cry?

SIR. H. Full cry!

LADY G. Ay! there is harmony, if you will. Give me the trumpet-
neigh; the spotted pack just catching scent. What a chorus is their
yelp! The view-hallo, blent with a peal of free and fearless mirth!
That's our old English music—match it where you can.

SIR H. (aside). I must see about Lady Gay Spanker.

DAZ. (aside to SIR HARCOURT). Ah, would you——

LADY G. Time then appears as young as love, and plumes as swift a
wing. Away we go! The earth flies back to aid our course! Horse,
man, hound, earth, heaven!—all—all—one piece of glowing ecstacy!
Then I love the world myself, and every living thing—my jocund soul
cries out for very glee, as it could wish that all creation had but one
mouth, that I might kiss it!

SIR H. (aside). I wish I were the mouth?

MAX. Why, we will regenerate you, Baronet! But Gay, where is
your husband? Where is Adolphus?

LADY G. Bless me, where is my Dolly?

SIR H. You are married, then?

LADY G. I have a husband somewhere, though I can't find him just
now. Dolly, dear! (aside to MAX) Governor, at home I always whistle
when I want him.

Enter Spanker, l.

Spanker. Here I am—did you call me, Gay?

Sir H. (*eyeing him*). Is that your husband?

Lady G. (*aside*). Yes, bless his stupid face, that's my Dolly.

Max. Permit me to introduce you to Sir Harcourt Courtley.

Span. How d'ye do? I—ah!—um! (*appears frightened.*)

Lady G. Delighted to have the honor of making the acquaintance of a gentleman so highly celebrated in the world of fashion.

Span. Oh, yes, delighted, I'm sure—quite—very, so delighted—delighted! (*gets quite confused, draws on his glove and tears it.*)

Lady G. Where have you been, Dolly?

Span. Oh, ah, I was just outside.

Max. Why did you not come in?

Span. I'm sure I didn't—I don't exactly know, but I thought as—perhaps—I can't remember.

Daz. Shall we have the pleasure of your company to dinner?

Span. I always dine—usually—that is, unless Gay remains——

Lady G. Stay dinner, of course; we came on purpose to stop three or four days with you.

Grace. Will you excuse my absence, Gay?

Max. What! what! Where are you going? What takes you away?

Grace. We must postpone the dinner till Gay is dressed.

Max. Oh, never mind,—stay where you are.

Grace. No, I must go.

Max. I say you sha'n't! I will be king in my own house.

Grace. Do, my dear uncle;—you shall be king, and I'll be your prime minister,—that is, I'll rule, and you shall have the honor of taking the consequences.   [*Exit, l.*

Lady G. Well said, Grace; have your own way, it is the only thing we women ought to be allowed.

Max. Come, Gay, dress for dinner.

Sir H. Permit me, Lady Gay Spanker.

Lady G. With pleasure,—what do you want?

Sir H. To escort you.

Lady G. Oh, never mind, I can escort myself, thank you, and Dolly too;—come, dear!   [*Exit, r.*

Sir H. Au revoir!

Span. Ah, thank you!   [*Exit, awkwardly, r.*

Sir H. What an ill-assorted pair!

Max. Not a bit! She married him for freedom, and she has it; he married her for protection, and he has it.

Sir H. How he ever summoned courage to propose to her, I can't guess.

Max. Bless you, he never did. She proposed to him. She says he would if he could; but as he couldn't, she did it for him.

[*Exit* Max *and* Sir H., *laughing, l.*

Enter Cool *with letter, l.*

Cool. Mr. Charles, I have been watching to find you alone. Sir Harcourt has written to town for you.

Young C. The devil he has!

Cool. He expects you down to-morrow evening.

Daz. Oh! he'll be punctual. A thought strikes me.

Young C. Pooh! Confound your thoughts! I can think of nothing

but the idea of leaving Grace, at the very moment when I had established the most——

Daz What if I can prevent her marriage with your governor?

Young C. Impossible!

Daz. He's pluming himself for the conquest of Lady Gay Spanker.
It will not be difficult to make him believe she accedes to his suit. And
if she would but join in the plan——

Young C. I see it all. And do you think she would?

Daz. I mistake my game if she would not.

Cool. Here comes Sir Harcourt!

Daz. I'll begin with him. Retire, and watch how I'll open the cam-
paign for you.   [Young Courtley and Cool retire.

Enter Sir Harcourt, l.

Sir H. Here is that cursed fellow again.

Daz. Ah, my dear old friend!

Sir H. Mr. Dazzle!

Daz. I have a secret of importance to disclose to you. Are you a
man of honor? Hush! don't speak; you are. It is with the greatest
pain I am compelled to request you, as a gentleman, that you will shun
studiously the society of Lady Gay Spanker!

Sir H. Good gracious! Wherefore, and by what right do you make
such a demand?

Daz. Why, I am distantly related to the Spankers.

Sir H. Why, damme, sir, if you don't appear to be related to every
family in Great Britain!

Daz. A good many of the nobility claim me as a connection. But, to
return—she is much struck with your address; evidently, she laid herself out for display——

Sir H. Ha! you surprise me!

Daz. To entangle you.

Sir H. Ha! ha! why, it did appear like it.

Daz. You will spare her for my sake; give her no encouragement;
if disgrace come upon my relatives, the Spankers, I should never hold
up my head again.

Sir H. (*aside*). I shall achieve an easy conquest, and a glorious.
Ha! ha! I never remarked it before, but this is a gentleman.

Daz. May I rely on your generosity?

Sir H. Faithfully. (*shakes his hand*) Sir, I honor and esteem you;
but, might I ask, how came you to meet our friend, Max Harkaway, in
my house in Belgrave Square?

Re-enter Young Courtley. *Sits on sofa at back,* l.

Daz. Certainly. I had an acceptance of your son's for one hundred
pounds.

Sir H. (*astonished*). Of my son's? Impossible!

Daz Ah, sir, fact! he paid a debt for a poor unfortunate man—
fifteen children—half-a-dozen wives—the devil knows what all.

Sir H. Simple boy.

Daz. Innocent youth, I have no doubt; when you have the hundred
convenient, I shall feel delighted.

Sir H. Oh! follow me to my room, and if you have the document, it
will be happiness to me to pay it. Poor Charles! good heart!

Daz. Oh, a splendid heart! I dare say. [*Exit* Sir Harcourt, l.
Come, here; write me the bill.

Young C. What for ?

Daz. What for ? why, to release the unfortunate man and his family, to be sure, from jail.

Young C. Who is he ?

Daz. Yourself.

Young C. But I haven't fifteen children !

Daz Will you take your oath of that !

Young C. Nor four wives.

Daz. More shame for you, with all that family. Come, don't be obstinate ; write and date it back.

Young C. Ah, but where is the stamp ?

Daz. Here they are, of all patterns. (*pulls out a pocket-book*) I keep them ready drawn in case of necessity, all but the date and acceptance. Now, if you are in an autographic humor, you can try how your signature will look across half-a-dozen of them ;—there—write—exactly— you know the place—across—good—and thank your lucky stars that you have found a friend at last, that gives you money and advice.

[*Takes paper and exit*, L.

Young C. Things are approaching to a climax ; I must appear in *propria persona*—and immediately—but I must first ascertain what are the real sentiments of this riddle of a woman. Does she love me ? I flatter myself—by Jove here she comes—I shall never have such an opportunity again !

Enter Grace, L.

Grace. I wish I had never seen Mr. Hamilton. Why does every object appear robbed of the charm it once presented to me ? Why do I shudder at the contemplation of this marriage, which, till now, was to me a subject of indifference ? Am I in love ? In love ! if I am, my past life has been the work of raising up a pedestal to place my own folly on—I—the infidel—the railer !

Young C. Meditating on matrimony, madam ?

Grace (*aside*). He little thinks he was the subject of my meditations ! (*aloud*) No.

Young C. (*aside*). I must unmask my battery now.

Grace (*aside*). How foolish I am—he will perceive that I tremble— I must appear at ease. (*a pause.*)

Young C. Eh ? ah ! um !

Grace. Ah ! (*they sink into silence again. Aside*) How very awkward !

Young C. (*aside*). It is a very difficult subject to begin. (*aloud*) Madam—ahem—there was—is—I mean—I was about to remark—a— (*aside*) Hang me if it is not a very slippery subject. I must brush up my faculties ; attack her in her own way. (*aloud*) Sing ! oh, muse ! (*aside*) Why, I have made love before to a hundred women !

Grace (*aside*). I wish I had something to do, for I have nothing to say.

Young C. Madam—there is—a subject so fraught with fate to my future life, that you must pardon my lack of delicacy should a too hasty expression mar the fervent courtesy of its intent. To you, I feel aware, I must appear in the light of a comparative stranger.

Grace (*aside*). I know what's coming.

Young C. Of you—I know perhaps too much for my own peace.

Grace (*aside*). He *is* in love.

Young C. I forget all that befell before I saw your beauteous self ; I seem born into another world—my nature changed—the beams of that bright face falling on my soul, have, from its chaos, warmed into life the flowrets of affection, whose maiden odors now float toward the sun, pouring forth on their pure tongue a mite of adoration, midst the voices of a universe. (*aside*) That's something in her own style.

GRACE. Mr. Hamilton!

YOUNG C. You cannot feel surprised——

GRACE. I am more than surprised. (*aside*) I am delighted.

YOUNG C. Do not speak so coldly.

GRACE. You have offended me.

YOUNG C. No, madam; no woman, whatever her state, can be offended by the adoration even of the meanest; it is myself whom I have offended and deceived—but still I ask your pardon.

GRACE (*aside*). Oh! he thinks I am refusing him. (*aloud*) I am not exactly offended, but——

YOUNG C. Consider my position—a few days—and an insurmountable barrier would have placed you beyond my wildest hopes—you would have been my mother.

GRACE. I should have been your mother! (*aside*) I thought so.

YOUNG C. No—that is. I meant Sir Harcourt Courtley's bride.

GRACE (*with great emphasis*). Never!

YOUNG C. How! never! may I then hope?—you turn away—you would not lacerate me by a refusal?

GRACE (*aside*). How stupid he is!

YOUNG C. Still silent! I thank you, Miss Grace—I ought to have expected this—fool that I have been—one course alone remains—farewell!

GRACE (*aside*). Now he's going.

YOUNG C. Farewell forever! (*sits*) Will you not speak one word? I shall leave this house immediately—I shall not see you again.

GRACE Unhand me, sir, I insist.

YOUNG C. (*aside*). Oh! what an ass I've been! (*rushes up to her and seizes her hand*) Release this hand? Never! never! (*kissing it*) Never will I quit this hand! it shall be my companion in misery—in solitude—when you are far away.

GRACE. Oh! should any one come! (*drops her handkerchief; he stoops to pick it up*) For Heaven's sake do not kneel.

YOUNG C. (*kneels*). Forever thus prostrate, before my soul's saint, I will lead a pious life of eternal adoration.

GRACE. Should we be discovered thus—pray, Mr. Hamilton—pray—pray.

YOUNG C. Pray! I am praying; what more can I do?

GRACE Your conduct is shameful.

YOUNG C. It is. (*rises.*)

GRACE. And if I do not scream, is it not for your sake—that—but it might alarm the family.

YOUNG C. It might—it would. Say, am I wholly indifferent to you? I entreat one word—I implore you—do not withdraw your hand. (*she snatches it away—he puts his arm around her waist*) You smile.

GRACE. Leave me, dear Mr. Hamilton!

YOUNG C. Dear! Then I am dear to you; that word once more; say —say you love me!

GRACE. Is this fair? (*he catches her in his arms and kisses her.*)

Enter LADY GAY SPANKER, R.

LADY G. Ha! oh!

GRACE. Gay! destruction!   [*Exit,* L.

YOUNG C. Fizgig! The devil!

LADY G. Don t mind me—pray, don't let me be any interruption !

YOUNG C. I was just——

LADY G. Yes, I see you were.

YOUNG C. Oh ! madam, how could you mar my bliss in the very ecstacy of its fulfillment ?

LADY G. I always like to be in at the death. Never drop you ears ; bless you, she is only a little fresh—give her her head, and she will outrun herself.

YOUNG C. Possibly ; but what am I to do ?

LADY G. Keep your seat.

YOUNG C But in a few days she will take a leap that must throw me —she marries Sir Harcourt Courtley.

LADY G. Why, that is awkward, certainly ; but you can challenge him, and shoot him.

YOUNG C. Unfortunately that is out of the question.

LADY G. How so ?

YOUNG C. You will not betray a secret, if I inform you ?

LADY G. All right—what is it ?

YOUNG C. I am his son.

LADY G. What—his son ? But he does not know you ?

YOUNG C. No ; I met him here by chance, and faced it out, I never saw him before in my life.

LADY G. Beautiful ! I see it all—you're in love with your mother that should be—your wife, that will be.

YOUNG C. Now, I think I could distance the old gentleman, if you will but lend us your assistance.

LADY G. I will in anything.

YOUNG C. You must know, then, that my father, Sir Harcourt, has fallen desperately in love with you.

LADY G. With me ! (*utters a scream of delight*) That is delicious !

YOUNG C. Now, if you only could——

LADY G. Could !—I will. Ha ! ha ! I see my cue. I'll cross his scent—I'll draw him after me. Ho ! ho ! won't I make love to him ? Ha !

YOUNG C. The only objection might be Mr. Spanker who might——

LADY G. No, he mightn't, he has no objection. Bless him, he's an inestimable little character—you don't know him as well as I do. I dare say—ha ! ha ! (*dinner-bell rings*) Here they come to dinner. I'll commence my operations on your governor immediately. Ha ! ha ! how I shall enjoy it.

YOUNG C. Be guarded !

Enter MAX HARKAWAY, SIR HARCOURT, DAZZLE, GRACE *and* SPANKER, L.

MAX. Now, gentlemen—Sir Harcourt, do you lead Grace.

LADY G. I believe Sir Harcourt is engaged to me. (*takes his arm.*)

MAX. Well, please yourselves.

They file out, MAX *first,* YOUNG COURTLEY *and* GRACE, SIR HARCOURT *coquetting with* LADY GAY, *leaving* DAZZLE. *who offers his arm to* SPANKER.

CURTAIN.

ACT IV.

SCENE.—*A handsome drawing-room in Oak Hall, chandeliers, tables with books, drawings, etc.* GRACE *and* LADY GAY *discovered.* SERVANT *handing coffee.*

GRACE. If there be one habit more abominable than another, it is that of the gentlemen sitting over their wine; it is a selfish, unfeeling fashion, and a gross insult to our sex.

LADY G. We are turned out just when the fun begins. How happy the poor wretches look at the contemplation of getting rid of us.

GRACE. The conventional signal for the ladies to withdraw is anxiously and deliberately waited for.

LADY G. Then I begin to wish I were a man.

GRACE. The instant the door is closed upon us, there rises a roar!

LADY G. In celebration of their short-lived liberty, my love; rejoicing over their emancipation.

GRACE. I think it very insulting, whatever it may be.

LADY G. Ah! my dear, philosophers say that man is the creature of an hour—it is the dinner hour, I suppose. (*loud noise. Cries of* " A song, a song.")

GRACE. I am afraid they are getting too pleasant to be agreeable.

LADY G. I hope the squire will restrict himself; after his third bottle he becomes rather voluminous. (*cries of* " Silence.") Some one is going to sing (*jumps up*) Let us hear! (SPANKER *is heard to sing.*)

GRACE. Oh, no, Gay, for Heaven's sake!

LADY G. Oho! ha! ha! why, that is my Dolly. (*at the conclusion of the verse*) Well, I never heard my Dolly sing before! Happy wretches, how I envy them!

Enter JAMES, L., *with a note.*

JAMES. Mr. Hamilton has just left the house for London.

GRACE. Impossible!—that is, without seeing—that is——

LADY G. Ha! ha!

GRACE. He never—speak, sir!

JAMES. He left, Miss Grace, in a desperate hurry, and this note, I believe, for you. (*presenting a note on salver.*)

GRACE. For me! (*about to snatch it, but restraining herself, takes it coolly.*)   [*Exit* JAMES.

(*Reads*) " Your manner during dinner has left me no alternative but instant departure; my absence will release you from the oppression which my society must necessarily inflict on your sensitive mind. It may tend also to smother, though it can never extinguish, that indomitable passion, of which I am the passive victim. Dare I supplicate pardon and oblivion for the past? It is the last request of the self-deceived, but still loving AUGUSTUS HAMILTON." (*puts her hand to her forehead and appears giddy.*)

LADY G. Hallo, Grace! what's the matter?

GRACE (*recovering herself*). Nothing—the heat of the room.

LADY G. Oh! what excuse does he make? particular unforeseen business, I suppose?

GRACE. Why, yes—a mere formula—a—a—you may put it in the fire. (*puts it in her bosom.*)

LADY G. (*aside*). It is near enough to the fire where it is.

GRACE. I'm glad he's gone.

LADY G. So am I.

GRACE. He was a disagreeble, ignorant person.

LADY G. Yes; and so vulgar.

GRACE. No, he was not at all vulgar.

LADY G. I mean in appearance.

GRACE. Oh! how can you so? he was very *distingue.*

LADY G. Well, I might have been mistaken, but I took him for a forward, intrusive——

GRACE. Good gracious, Gay! he was very retiring—even shy.

LADY G. (*aside*). It's all right. *She* is in love,—blows hot and cold in the same breath.

GRACE. How can you be a competent judge? Why, you have not known him more than a few hours,—while I—I——

LADY G. Have known him two days and a quarter! I yield—I confess, I never was, or will be so intimate with him as you appeared to be ! Ha! ha! (*loud noise of argument. The folding-doors are thrown open.*)

Enter the whole party of GENTLEMEN, *apparently engaged in warm discussion. They assemble in knots, while the* SERVANTS *hand coffee, etc.* MAX, SIR HARCOURT, DAZZLE, *and* SPANKER, *together.*

DAZ. But, my dear sir, consider the position of the two countries. under such a constitution.

SIR H. The two countries! What have they to do with the subject.

MAX. Everything. Look at their two legislative bodies.

SPAN. Ay, look at their two legislative bodies.

SIR H. Why, it would inevitably establish universal anarchy and confusion.

GRACE. I think that they are pretty well established already.

SPAN. Well, suppose it did, what has anarchy and confusion to do with the subject?

LADY G. Do look at my Dolly : he is arguing—talking politics—'pon my life he is. (*calling*) Mr. Spanker, my dear !

SPAN. Excuse me, love, I am discussing a point of importance.

LADY G. Oh, that is delicious ; he must discuss that to me. (*she goes up and leads him down, he appears to have shaken off his gaucherie, she shakes her head*) Dolly ! Dolly !

SPAN. Pardon me, Lady Gay Spanker, I conceive your mutilation of my sponsorial appellation derogatory to my *amour propre.*

LADY G. Your what? Ho! ho!

SPAN. And I particularly request that, for the future, I may not be treated with that cavalier spirit which does not become your sex nor your station, your ladyship.

LADY G. You have been indulging till you have lost the little wit nature dribbled into your unfortunate little head—your brains want the whipper-in—you are not yourself.

SPAN. Madam, I am doubly myself ; and permit me to inform you, that unless you voluntarily pay obedience to my commands, I shall enforce them.

LADY G. Your commands !

SPAN. Yes, madam ; I mean to put a full stop to your hunting.

LADY G. You do! ah! (*aside*) I can scarcely speak from delight. (*aloud*) Who put such an idea into your head, for I am sure it is not an original emanation of your genius?

SPAN. Sir Harcourt Courtley, my friend ; and now, mark me! I request, for your own sake, that I may not be compelled to assert my a—my authority, as your husband. I shall say no more than this—if you persist in your absurd rebellion——

LADY G. Well?

SPAN. Contemplate a separation.

[Looks at her haughtily and retires.

LADY G. Now I'm happy! My own little darling, inestimable Dolly, has tumbled into a spirit, somehow. Sir Harcourt, too! Ha! ha! he's trying to make him ill-treat me, so that his own suit may thrive.

SIR H. (*advances*). Lady Gay!

LADY G. Now for it.

SIR H. What hours of misery were those I passed, when, by your secession, the room suffered a total eclipse.

LADY G. Ah! you flatter.

SIR H. No, pardon me, that were impossible. No, believe me, I tried to join in the boisterous mirth, but my thoughts would desert to the drawing-room. Ah! how I envied the careless levity and cool indifference with which Mr. Spanker enjoyed your absence.

DAZ. (*who is lounging in a chair*). Max, that Madeira is worth its weight in gold; I hope you have more of it.

MAX. A pipe, I think.

DAZ. I consider a magnum of that nectar, and a meerschaum of kanaster, to consummate the ultimatum of all mundane bliss. To drown myself in liquid ecstacy, and then blow a cloud on which the enfranchised soul could soar above Olympus. Oh!

Enter JAMES, L.

JAMES. Mr. Charles Courtley!

SIR H. Ah, now, Max, you must see a living apology for my conduct.

Enter YOUNG COURTLEY, *dressed very plainly.*

Well, Charles, how are you? Don't be afraid. There, Max, what do you say now?

MAX. Well, this is the most extraordinary likeness.

GRACE (*aside*). Yes—considering it is the original. I am not so easily deceived!

MAX. Sir, I am delighted to see you.

YOUNG C. Thank you, sir.

DAZ. Will you be kind enough to introduce me, Sir Harcourt?

SIR H. This is Mr. Dazzle, Charles.

YOUNG C. Which? (*looking from* SPANKER *to* DAZZLE)

SIR H. (*to* LADY GAY) Is not that refreshing? Miss Harkaway— Charles, this is your mother, or rather will be.

YOUNG C. Madam, I shall love, honor, and obey you punctually. (*takes out book, sighs, and goes up reading.*)

Enter JAMES, L.

SIR H. You perceive? Quite unused to society—perfectly ignorant of every conventional rule of life.

JAMES. The doctor and the young ladies have arrived. [*Exit*, L.

MAX. The young ladies—now we must to the ball—I make it a rule always to commence the festivities with a good old country dance—a rattling Sir Roger de Coverly; come, Sir Harcourt.

Sir H. Does this antiquity require a war-whoop in it?

Max. Nothing but a nimble foot and a light heart.

Sir H. Very antediluvian indispensables! Lady Gay Spanker, will you honor me by becoming my preceptor?

Lady G. Why, I am engaged—but (*aloud*) on such a plea as Sir Harcourt's, I must waive all obstacles.

Max. Now, Grace, girl—give your hand to Mr. Courtley.

Grace. Pray, excuse me, uncle—I have a headache.

Sir H. (*aside*). Jealousy! by the gods. Jealous of my devotions at another's fane! (*aloud*) Charles, my boy! amuse Miss Grace during our absence.   [*Exit, with* Lady Gay, L.

Max. But don't you dance, Mr. Courtley?

Young C. Dance, sir!—I never dance—I can procure exercise in a much more rational manner—and music disturbs my meditations.

Max. Well, do the gallant.   [*Exit*, L.

Young C. I never studied that art—but I have a Prize Essay on a hydrostatic subject, which would delight her—for it enchanted the Reverend Doctor Pump, of Corpus Christi.

Grace (*aside*). What on earth could have induced him to disguise himself in that frightful way!—I rather suspect some plot to entrap me into a confession.

Young C. (*aside*). Dare I confess this trick to her? No! Not until I have proved her affection indisputably. Let me see—I must concoct. (*takes a chair, and forgetting his assumed character, is about to take his natural free manner.* Grace *looks surprised. He turns abashed*) Madam, I have been desired to amuse you.

Grace. Thank you.

Young C. "The labor we delight in, physics pain." I will draw you a moral, ahem! Subject, the effects of inebriety!—which, according to Ben Jonson—means perplexion of the intellects, caused by imbibing spirituous liquors. About an hour before my arrival, I passed an appalling evidence of the effects of this state—a carriage was overthrown—horses killed—gentleman in a hopeless state, with his neck broken—all occasioned by the intoxication of the post-boy.

Grace. That is very amusing.

Young C. I found it edifying—nutritious food for reflection—the expiring man desired his best compliments to you.

Grace. To me?

Young C. Yes.

Grace. His name was——

Young C. Mr. Augustus Hamilton.

Grace. Augustus! Oh! (*affects to faint.*)

Young C. (*aside*). Huzza!

Grace. But where, sir, did this happen?

Young C. About four miles down the road.

Grace. He must be conveyed here.

Enter Servant, L.

Serv. Mr. Meddle, madam.   [*Exit*, L.

Enter Meddle, L.

Med. On very particular business.

Grace. The very person. My dear sir!

Med. My dear madam!

Grace. You must execute a very particular commission for me immediately. Mr. Hamilton has met with a frightful accident on the London road, and is in a dying state.

MED. Well! I have no hesitation in saying, he takes it uncommonly easy—he looks as if he was used to it.

GRACE. You mistake; that is not Mr. Hamilton, but Mr. Courtley, who will explain everything, and conduct you to the spot.

YOUNG C. (aside). Oh! I must put a stop to all this, or I shall be found out. (aloud) Madam, that were useless, for I omitted to mention a small fact which occurred before I left Mr. Hamilton—he died.

GRACE. Dear me! Oh, then we needn't trouble you, Mr. Meddle. (music heard) Hark! I hear they are commencing a waltz—if you will ask me—perhaps your society and conversation may tend to dispel the dreadful sensations you have aroused.

YOUNG C. (aside). Hears of my death—screams out—and then asks me to waltz! I am bewildered! Can she suspect me? I wonder which she likes best—me or my double? Confound this disguise—I must retain it—I have gone too far with my dad to pull up now. (aloud) At your service, madam.

GRACE (aside). I will pay him well for this trick!

[Exeunt, L., all but MEDDLE.

MED. Well, if that is not Mr. Hamilton, scratch me out with a big blade, for I am a blot—a mistake upon the rolls. There is an error in the pleadings somewhere, and I will discover it. I would swear to his identity before the most discriminating jury. By the bye, this accident will form a capital excuse for my presence here. I just stepped in to see how matters worked, and—stay—here comes the bridegroom elect—and, oh! in his very arms, Lady Gay Spanker! (looks round) Where are my witnesses? Oh, that some one else were here! However I can retire and get some information, eh—Spanker versus Courtley—damages—witness. (gets into an arm-chair, which he turns round.)

Enter SIR HARCOURT COURTLEY, *supporting* LADY GAY, L.

SIR H. This cool room will recover you.

LADY G. Excuse my trusting to you for support.

SIR H. I am transported! Allow me thus ever to support this lovely burden, and I shall conceive that paradise is regained. (they sit.)

LADY G. Oh! Sir Harcourt, I feel very faint.

SIR H. The waltz made you giddy.

LADY G. And I have left my salts in the other room.

SIR H. I always carry a flacon, for the express accommodation of the fair sex. (producing a smelling-bottle.)

LADY G. Thank you—ah! (she sighs,)

SIR H. What a sigh was there!

LADY G. The vapor of consuming grief.

SIR H. Grief? Is it possible! Have you a grief? Are you unhappy? Dear me!

LADY G. Am I not married?

SIR H. What a horrible state of existence!

LADY G. I am never contradicted, so there are none of those enlivening, interesting little differences, which so pleasingly diversify the monotony of conjugal life, like spots of verdure—no quarrels, like oases in the desert of matrimony—no rows.

SIR H. How vulgar! what a brute!

LADY G. I never have anything but my own way; and he won't permit me to spend more than I like.

SIR H. Mean-spirited wretch!

LADY G. How can I help being miserable?

SIR H Miserable! I wonder you are not in a lunatic asylum, with such unheard-of barbarity!

LADY G. But worse than all that!

SIR H. Can it be out-Heroded?

LADY G. Yes, I could forgive that—I do—it is my duty. But only imagine—picture to yourself, my dear Sir Harcourt, though I, the third daughter of an Earl, married him out of pity for his destitute and helpless situation as a bachelor with ten thousand a year—conceive, if you can—he actually permits me, with the most placid indifference, to flirt with any old fool I may meet.

SIR H. Good gracious! miserable idiot!

LADY G. I fear there is an incompatability of temper, which renders a separation inevitable.

SIR H. Indispensable, my dear madam! Ah! had I been the happy possessor of such a realm of bliss—what a beatific eternity unfolds itself to my extending imagination! Had another man but looked at you, I should have annihilated him at once; and if he had the temerity to speak, his life alone could have expiated his crime.

LADY G. Oh, an existence of such a nature is too bright for the eye of thought—too sweet to bear reflection.

SIR H. My devotion, eternal, deep——

LADY G. Oh, Sir Harcourt!

SIR H. (more fervently). Your every thought should be a separate study—each wish forestalled by the quick apprehension of a kindred soul.

LADY G. Alas! how can I avoid my fate?

SIR H. If a life—a heart—were offered to your astonished view by one who is considered the index of fashion—the vane of the *beau monde*—if you saw him at your feet begging, beseeching your acceptance of all, and more than this, what would your answer——

LADY G. Ah! I know of none so devoted!

SIR H. You do! (*throwing himself upon his knees*) Behold Sir Harcourt Courtley! (MEDDLE *jumps up into the chair.*)

LADY G. (*aside*). Ha! ha! Yoicks! Puss has broken cover.

SIR H. Speak, adored, dearest Lady Gay!—speak—will you fly from the tyranny, the wretched misery of such a monster's roof, and accept the soul which lives but in your presence!

LADY G. Do not press me. Oh, spare a weak, yielding woman—be contented to know that you are, alas! too dear to me. But the world —the world would say——

SIR H. Let us be a precedent to open a more extended and liberal view of matrimonial advantages to society

LADY G. How irresistible is your argument! Oh! pause!

SIR H. I have ascertained for a fact, that every tradesman of mine lives with his wife, and thus you see it has become a vulgar and plebeian custom.

LADY G. Leave me; I feel I cannot withstand your powers of persuasion. Swear that you will never forsake me.

SIR H. Dictate the oath May I grow wrinkled—may two inches be added to the circumference of my waist—may I lose the fall in my back—may I be old and ugly the instant I forego one tithe of adoration!

LADY G I must believe you.

SIR H. Shall we leave this detestable spot—this horrible vicinity?

LADY G. The sooner the better; to-morrow evening let it be. Now let me return; my absence will be remarked. (*he kisses her hand*) Do

I appear confused? Has my agitation rendered me unfit to enter
the room?

Sir H. More angelic by a lovely tinge of heightened color.

Lady G. To-morrow, in this room, which opens on the lawn.

Sir H. At eleven o'clock.

Lady G. Have your carriage in waiting, and four horses. Remember, please be particular to have four; don't let the affair come off
shabbily. Adieu, dear Sir Harcourt!　　　　　　　　　[Exit, L.

Sir H. Veni, vidi, vici! Hannibal, Cæsar, Napoleon, Alexander never
completed so fair a conquest in so short a time. She dropped fasci-
nated. This is an unprecedented example of the irresistible force of
personal appearance combined with polished address. Poor creature!
how she loves me! I pity so prostrating a passion, and ought to return it. I will; it is a duty I owe to society and fashion.　[Exit, L.

Med. (turns the chair round). "There is a tide in the affairs of men,
which, taken at the flood, leads on to fortune." This is my tide—I am
the only witness. "Virtue is sure to find its own reward." But I've
no time to contemplate what I shall be—something huge. Let me see
—Spanker *versus* Courtley—Crim. Con. Damages placed at £150,000
at least, for juries always decimate your hopes.

Enter Spanker, L.

Span. I cannot find Gay anywhere.

Med. The plaintiff himself—I must commence the action. Mr. Spanker, as I have information of deep vital importance to impart, will you
take a seat? (they sit solemnly. Meddle takes out a note-book and
pencil) Ahem! You have a wife?

Re-enter Lady Gay *behind*, L.

Span. Yes, I believe I——

Med. Will you be kind enough, without any prevarication, to answer
my questions?

Span. You alarm—I——

Med. Compose yourself and reserve your feelings; take time to consider. You have a wife?

Span. Yes——

Med. He has a wife—good—a *bona-fide* wife—bound morally and
legally to be your wife, and nobody else's in effect, except on your
written permission——

Span. But what has this——

Med. Hush! allow me, my dear sir, to congratulate you. (shakes his
hand.)

Span. What for?

Med. Lady Gay Spanker is about to dishonor the bond of wedlock
by eloping from you.

Span. (starting). What?

Med. Be patient—I thought you would be overjoyed. Place the
affair in my hands, and I will venture to promise the largest damages
on record.

Span. D—n the damages!—I want my wife. Oh, I'll go and ask her
not to run away. She may run away with me—she may hunt—she
may ride—anything she likes. Oh, sir, let us put a stop to this affair.

Med. Put a stop to it! do not alarm me, sir. Sir, you will spoil the
most exquisite brief that was ever penned. It must proceed—it shall

proceed. It is illegal to prevent it, and I will bring an action against you for wilful intent to injure the profession.

SPAN. Oh, what an ass I am! Oh, I have driven her to this. It was all that d—d brandy punch on the top of Burgundy. What a fool I was!

MED. It was the happiest moment of your life. ·

SPAN. So I thought at the time; but we live to grow wiser. Tell me, who is this vile seducer?

MED. Sir Harcourt Courtley.

SPAN. Ha! he is my best friend.

MED. I should think he is. If you will accompany me—here is a verbatim copy of the whole transaction in short-hand—sworn to by me.

SPAN. Only let me have Gay back again.

MED. Even that may be arranged—this way.

SPAN. That ever I should live to see my wife run away. Oh, I will do anything—keep two packs of hounds—buy up every horse and ass in England—myself included—oh! [*Exit* SPANKER *and* MEDDLE, L.

LADY G. Ha! ha! ha! Poor Dolly! I'm sorry I must continue to deceive him. If he would kindle up a little. So, that fellow overheard all—well, so much the better.

Enter YOUNG COURTLEY, R.

YOUNG C. My dear madam, how fares the plot? does my governor nibble?

LADY G. Nibble! he is caught and in the basket. I have just left him with a hook in his gills, panting for very lack of element. But how goes on your encounter?

YOUNG C. Bravely. By a simple ruse, I have discovered that she loves me. I see but one chance against the best termination I could hope.

LADY G. What is that?

YOUNG C. My father has told me that I return to town again to-morrow afternoon.

LADY G. Well, I insist you stop and dine—keep out of the way.

YOUNG C. Oh, but what excuse shall I offer for disobedience? What can I say when he sees me before dinner?

LADY G. Say—say Grace.

Enter GRACE, L., *and gets behind the window curtains.*

YOUNG C. Ha! ha!

LADY G. I have arranged to elope with Sir Harcourt myself to-morrow night.

YOUNG C. The deuce you have!

LADY G. Now if you could persuade Grace to follow that example—his carriage will be waiting at the Park—be there a little before eleven, and it will just prevent our escape. Can you make her agree to that?

YOUNG C. Oh, without the slightest difficulty, if Mr. Augustus Hamilton supplicates.

LADY G. Success attend you. (*going.*)

YOUNG C. I will bend the haughty Grace. (*going.*)

LADY G. Do.   [*Exeunt severally.*

GRACE. Will you?

CURTAIN.

ACT V.

SCENE.—*A drawing-room in Oak Hall.*

Enter COOL, L.

COOL. This is the most serious affair Sir Harcourt has ever been engaged in. I took the liberty of considering him a fool when he told me he was going to marry; but voluntarily to incur another man's incumbrance is very little short of madness. If he continues to conduct himself in this absurd manner, I shall be compelled to dismiss him.

Enter SIR HARCOURT, L., *equipped for travelling.*

SIR H. Cool!

COOL. Sir Harcourt.

SIR H. Is my chariot in waiting?

COOL. For the last half hour at the park wicket. But, pardon the insinuation, sir; would it not be more advisable to hesitate a little for a short reflection before you undertake the heavy responsibility of a woman?

SIR H. No; hesitation destroys the romance of a *faux pas*, and reduces it to the level of a mere mercantile calculation.

COOL. What is to be done with Mr. Charles?

SIR H. Ay, much against my will, Lady Gay prevailed on me to permit him to remain. You, Cool, must return him to college. Pass through London, and deliver these papers; here is a small notice of the coming elopement for the Morning Post; this, by an eye-witness, for the Herald; this, with all the particulars, for the Chronicle; and the full and circumstantial account for the evening journals—after which, meet us at Boulogne.

COOL. Very good, Sir Harcourt. (*going.*)

SIR H. Lose no time. Remember—Hotel Anglais, Boulogne-sur-Mer. And, Cool, bring a few copies with you, and don't forget to distribute some amongst very particular friends.

COOL. It shall be done.   [*Exit,* L.

" SIR H. With what indifference does a man of the world view the approach of the most perilous catastrophe! My position, hazardous as it is, entails none of that nervous excitement which a neophyte in the school of fashion would feel. I am as cool and steady as possible. Habit, habit! Oh! how many roses will fade upon the cheek of beauty when the defalcation of Sir Harcourt Courtley is whispered—then hinted—at last, confirmed and bruited. I think I see them. Then, on my return, they will not dare to eject me—I am their sovereign! Whoever attempts to think of treason, I'll banish him from the West End—I'll cut him—I'll put him out of fashion!"

Enter LADY GAY, L.

LADY G. Sir Harcourt!

SIR H. At your feet.

LADY G. I had hoped you would have repented.

SIR H. Repented!

LADY G. Have you not come to say it was a jest?—say you have!

SIR H. Love is too sacred a subject to be trifled with. Come, let us fly! See, I have procured disguises——

LADY G. My courage begins to fail me.   Let me return.

SIR H. Impossible!

LADY G. Where do you intend to take me?

SIR H. You shall be my guide.   The carriage waits.

LADY G. You will never desert me?

SIR H. Desert! Oh, Heavens! Nay, do not hesitate—flight, now, alone is left to your desperate situation! Come, every moment is laden with danger. (*they are going.*)

LADY G. Oh! gracious!

SIR H. Hush! what is it?

LADY G. I have forgotten—I must return.

SIR H. Impossible!

LADY G I must! I must! I have left Max—a pet staghound, in his basket—without whom life would be unendurable—I could not exist!

SIR H. No, no.   Let him be sent after us in a hamper.

LADY G. In a hamper! Remorseless man! Go—you love me not. How would you like to be sent after me—in a hamper? Let me fetch him.   Hark! I hear him squeal! Oh! Max—Max!

SIR H. Hush! for Heaven's sake.   They'll imagine you're calling the Squire.   I hear footsteps; where can I retire? (*goes up,* R.)

Enter MEDDLE, SPANKER, DAZZLE, *and* MAX, L.   LADY GAY *screams.*

MED. Spanker versus Courtley!—I subpœna every one of you as witnesses!—I have 'em ready—here they are—shilling a-piece. (*giving them round.*)

LADY G. Where is Sir Harcourt?

MED. There!—bear witness!—call on the vile delinquent for protection!

SPAN. Oh! his protection!

LADY G. What? ha!

MED. I'll swear I overheard the whole elopement planned—before any jury!—where's the book?

SPAN. Do you hear, you profligate?

LADY G. Ha! ha! ha! ha!

DAZ. But where is this wretched Lothario?

MED. Ay, where is the defendant?

SPAN. Where lies the hoary villain?

LADY G. What villain?

SPAN. That will not serve you!—I'll not be blinded that way!

MED. We won't be blinded any way!

MAX. I must seek Sir Harcourt, and demand an explanation! Such a thing never occurred in Oak Hall before—it must be cleared up!

[*Exit,* R.

MED. (*aside to* SPANKER). Now, take my advice; remember your gender.   Mind the notes I have given you.

SPAN. (*aside*). All right! Here they are! Now, madam, I have procured the highest legal opinion on this point.

MED. Hear! hear!

SPAN. And the question resolves itself into a—into—What's this? (*looks at notes.*)

MED. A nutshell!

SPAN. Yes, we are in a nutshell.   Will you, in every respect, subscribe to my requests—desires—commands—(*looks at notes*)—orders—imperative—indicative—injunctive—or otherwise?

LADY G. (*aside*). 'Pon my life, he's actually going to assume the ribbons, and take the box-seat. I must put a stop to this. I will! It will all end in smoke. I know Sir Harcourt would rather run than fight!

DAZ. Oh! I smell powder!—command my services. My dear madam, can I be of any use?

SPAN. Oh! a challenge! I must consult my legal adviser.

MED No! impossible!

DAZ. Pooh! the easiest thing in life! Leave it to me. What has an attorney to do with affairs of honor?—they are out of his element.

MED. Compromise the question? Pull his nose!—we have no objection to that.

DAZ. (*turning to* LADY GAY). Well, we have no objection either—have we?

LADY G. No!—pull his nose—that will be something.

MED. And, moreover, it is not exactly actionable!

DAZ. Isn't it!—thank you—I'll note down that piece of information—it may be useful.

MED. How! cheated out of my legal knowledge?

LADY G. Mr. Spanker, I am determined!—I insist upon a challenge being sent to Sir Harcourt Courtley!—and—mark me—if you refuse to fight him—I will.

MED. Don't; take my advice—you'll incapacit——

LADY G. Look you, Mr. Meddle, unless you wish me to horsewhip you, hold your tongue.

MED. What a she-tiger—I shall retire and collect my costs.

                                             [*Exit* L.

LADY G. Mr. Spanker, oblige me by writing as I dictate.

SPAN. He's gone—and now I am defenceless! Is this the fate of husbands!—a duel! Is this the result of becoming master of my own family?

LADY G. "Sir, the situation in which you were discovered with my wife, admits neither of explanation nor apology."

SPAN. Oh, yes! but it does—I don't believe you really intended to run quite away.

LADY G. You do not; but I know better, I say I did! and if it had not been for your unfortunate interruption, I do not know where I might have been by this time. Go on.

SPAN. " Nor apology." I'm writing my own death-warrant—committing suicide on compulsion.

LADY G. " The bearer will arrange all preliminary matters; for another day must see this sacrilege expiated by your life, or that of yours very sincerely, DOLLY SPANKER." Now, Mr. Dazzle. (*gives it over his head*)

DAZ. The document is as sacred as if it were a hundred pound bill.

LADY G. We trust to your discretion.

SPAN. His discretion! Oh, put your head in a tiger's mouth, and trust to his discretion!

DAZ. (*sealing letter, etc., with* SPANKER'S *seal*). My dear Lady Gay, matters of this kind are indigenous to my nature, independently of their pervading fascination to all humanity; but this is the more especially delightful, as you may perceive I shall be the intimate and bosom friend of both parties.

LADY G. Is it not the only alternative in such a case?

DAZ. It is a beautiful panacea in any, in every case. (*going—returns*) By the way, where would you like this party of pleasure to come off? Open air shooting is pleasant enough, but if I might venture to advise, we could order half-a-dozen of that Madeira and a box of cigars into

the billiard-room, so make a night of it; take up the irons every now
and then; string for first shot, and blaze away at one another in an
amicable and gentlemanlike way; so conclude the matter before the
protency of the liquor could disturb the individuality of the object, or
the smoke of the cigars render the outline dubious. Does such an ar-
rangement coincide with your views?

LADY G. Perfectly.

DAZ. I trust shortly to be the harbinger of happy tidings.

[*Exit*, L.

SPAN. (*coming forward*). Lady Gay Spanker, are you ambitious of
becoming a widow?

LADY G. Why, Dolly, woman is at best but weak, and weeds become
me.

SPAN. Female! am I to be immolated on the altar of your vanity?

LADY G. If you become pathetic, I shall laugh.

SPAN. Farewell—base, heartless, unfeeling woman!   [*Exit*, L.

LADY G. Ha! well, so I am. I am heartless, for he is a dear, good
little fellow, and I ought not to play upon his feelings; but 'pon my life
he sounds so well up at concert pitch, that I feel disinclined to untune
him. *Poor Doll, I didn't think he cared so much about me.*   I will
put him out of pain.   [*Exit*, L. SIR HARCOURT *comes down.*

SIR H. I have been a fool! a dupe to my own vanity. I shall be
pointed at as a ridiculous old coxcomb—and so I am. The hour of conviction is *arrived.* Have I deceived myself? Have I turned all my
senses inwards—looking towards self—always self?—and has the world
been ever laughing at me? Well, if they have, I will revert the joke;
they may say I am an old ass; but I will prove that I am neither too
old to repent my folly, nor such an ass as to flinch from confessing it.
A blow half met is but half felt.

Enter DAZZLE, L.

DAZ. Sir Harcourt, may I be permitted the honor of a few minutes'
conversation with you?

SIR H. With pleasure.

DAZ. Have the kindness to throw your eye over that. (*gives letter.*)

SIR H. (*reads*). ' Situation—my wife—apology—expiate—my life.''
Why, this is intended for a challenge.

DAZ. Why, indeed, I am perfectly aware that it is not quite *en regle*
in the couching, for with that I had nothing to do; but I trust that the
irregularity of the composition will be confounded in the beauty of the
subject.

SIR H. Mr. Dazzle, are you in earnest?

DAZ. Sir Harcourt Courtley, upon my honor I am, and I hope that
no previous engagement will interfere with an immediate reply in *propria persona.* We have fixed upon the billiard room as the scene of
action, which have just seen properly illuminated in honor of the occasion! and, by the bye, if your implements are not handy, I can oblige
you with a pair of the sweetest things you ever handled—hair-trig-
gered—saw grip; heir-looms in my family. I regard them almost in
the light of relations.

SIR H. Sir, I shall avail myself of one of your relatives. (*aside*) One
of the hereditaments of my folly—I must accept it. (*aloud*) Sir, I shall
be happy to meet Mr. Spanker at any time or place he may appoint.

DAZ. The sooner the better, sir. Allow me to offer you my arm. I
see you understand these matters;—my friend Spanker is wofully ignorant—miserably uneducated.   [*Exeunt*, L.

Re-enter MAX, *with* GRACE, R.

MAX. Give ye joy, girl, give ye joy. Sir Harcourt Courtley must consent to waive all title to your hand in favor of his son Charles.

GRACE. Oh, indeed! Is that the pitch of your congratulation—humph! the exchange of an old fool for a young one? Pardon me if I am not able to distinguish the advantage.

MAX Advantage!

GRACE. Moreover, by what right am I a transferable cipher in the family of Courtley? So, then, my fate is reduced to this, to sacrifice my fortune, or unite myself with a worm-eaten edition of the Classics!

MAX. Why, he certainly is not such a fellow as I could have chosen for my little Grace; but consider, to retain fifteen thousand a-year! Now, tell me honestly—but why should I say *honestly?* Speak, girl, would you rather not have the lad?

GRACE. Why do you ask me?

MAX. Why, look ye, I'm an old fellow; another hunting season or two, and I shall be in at my own death—I can't leave you this house and land, because they are entailed, nor can I say I am sorry for it, for it is a good law; but I have a little box with my Grace's name upon it, where, since your father's death and miserly will, I have yearly placed a certain sum to be yours, should you refuse to fulfill the conditions prescribed.

GRACE. My own dear uncle! (*clasping him round the neck.*)

MAX. Pooh! pooh! what's to do now? Why, it was only a trifle—why, you little rogue, what are you crying about?

GRACE. Nothing, but——

MAX. But what? Come, out with it. Will you have young Courtley?

Re-enter LADY GAY, L.

LADY G. Oh! Max, Max!

MAX. Why, what's amiss with you?

LADY G. I'm a wicked woman!

MAX. What have you done?

LADY G. Everything—oh, I thought Sir Harcourt was a coward, but now I find a man may be a coxcomb without being a poltroon. Just to show my husband how inconvenient it is to hold the ribands sometimes, I made him send a challenge to the old fellow, and he, to my surprise, accepted it, and is going to blow my Dolly's brains out in the billiard-room.

MAX. The devil!

LADY G. Just when I imagined I had got my whip hand of him again, out comes my linch-pin—and over I go—oh!

MAX. I will soon put a stop to that—a duel under my roof! Murder in Oak Hall! I'll shoot them both!   [*Exit*, L.

GRACE. Are you really in earnest?

LADY G. Do you think it looks like a joke? Oh! Dolly, if you allow yourself to be shot, I will never forgive you—never! Ah, he is a great fool, Grace! but I can't tell why, I would sooner lose my bridle hand than he should be hurt on my account. (*two shots are fired without*, L.)

Enter SIR HARCOURT, L.

Tell me—tell me—have you shot him—is he dead—my dear Sir Harcourt? You horrid old brute—have you killed him? I shall never forgive myself.   [*Exit*, L.

GRACE. Oh! Sir Harcourt, what has happened?

SIR H. Don't be alarmed, I beg—your uncle interrupted us—discharged the weapons—locked the challenger up in the billiard-room to cool his rage.

GRACE. Thank Heaven!

SIR H. Miss Grace, to apologize for my conduct were useless, more especially as I am confident that no feelings of indignation or sorrow for my late acts are cherished by you; but still, reparation is in my power, and I not only waive all title, right, or claim to your person or your fortune, but freely admit your power to bestow them on a more worthy object.

GRACE. This generosity, Sir Harcourt, is most unexpected.

SIR H. No, not generosity, but simple justice, justice!

GRACE. May I still beg a favor?

SIR H. Claim anything that is mine to grant.

GRACE. You have been duped by Lady Gay Spanker, I have also been cheated and played upon by her and Mr. Hamilton—may I beg that the contract between us, may, to all appearances, be still held good?

SIR H. Certainly, although I confess I cannot see the point of your purpose.

Enter MAX, *with* YOUNG COURTLEY, L.

MAX. Now, Grace, I have brought the lad.

GRACE. Thank you, uncle, but the trouble was quite unnecessary—Sir Harcourt holds to his original contract.

MAX. The deuce he does!

GRACE. And I am willing—nay, eager, to become Lady Courtley.

YOUNG C. (*aside*). The deuce you are!

MAX. But, Sir Harcourt——

SIR H. One word, Max, for an instant. (*they retire*, L.)

YOUNG C. (*aside*). What can this mean? Can it be possible that I have been mistaken—that she is not in love with Augustus Hamilton?

GRACE. Now we shall find how he intends to bend the haughty Grace.

YOUNG C. Madam—Miss, I mean—are you really in earnest—are you in love with my father?

GRACE. No, indeed I am not.

YOUNG C. Are you in love with any one else?

GRACE. No, or I should not marry him.

YOUNG C. Then you actually accept him as your real husband?

GRACE. In the common acceptation of the word.

YOUNG C. (*aside*). Hang me if I have not been a pretty fool! (*aloud*) Why do you marry him, if you don't care about him?

GRACE. To save my fortune.

YOUNG C. (*aside*). Mercenary, cold-hearted girl! (*aloud*) But if there be any one you love in the least—marry him. Were you never in love?

GRACE. Never!

YOUNG C. (*aside*). Oh! what an ass I've been! (*aloud*) I heard Lady Gay mention something about a Mr. Hamilton.

GRACE. Ah, yes, a person who, after an acquaintanceship of two days, had the assurance to make love to me, and I——

YOUNG C. Yes—you—well?

GRACE. I pretended to receive his attentions.

YOUNG C. (*aside*). It was the best pretence I ever saw.

GRACE. An absurd, vain, conceited coxcomb, who appeared to imagine that I was so struck with his fulsome speech that he could turn me around his finger.

YOUNG C. (*aside*). My very thoughts!

GRACE. But he was mistaken.

YOUNG C. (*aside*). Confoundedly! (*aloud*) Yet you seemed rather concerned about the news of his death.

GRACE. His accident? No, but——

YOUNG C. But what?

GRACE. (*aside*). What can I say? (*aloud*) Ah! but my maid Pert's brother is a post-boy, and I thought he might have sustained an injury, poor boy.

YOUNG C. (*aside*). D—n the post-boy! (*aloud*) Madam, if the retention of your fortune be the plea on which you are about to bestow your hand on the one you do not love, and whose very actions speak his carelessness for that inestimable jewel he is incapable of appreciating—know that I am devotedly, madly attached to you.

GRACE. You, sir? Impossible!

YOUNG C. Not at all—but inevitable—I have been so for a long time.

GRACE. Why, you never saw me until last night.

YOUNG C. I have seen you in imagination—you are the ideal I have worshipped.

GRACE. Since you press me into a confession—which nothing but this could bring me to speak—know, I did love poor Augustus Hamilton—

Re-enter MAX *and* SIR HARCOURT.

but he—he is—no—more! Pray, spare me, sir.

YOUNG C. (*aside*). She loves me! And, oh! what a situation I am in!—if I own I am the man, my governor will overhear, and ruin me—if I do not, she'll marry him. What is to be done?

Enter LADY GAY, L.

LADY G. Where have you put my Dolly? I have been racing all round the house—tell me, is he quite dead!

MAX. I'll have him brought in.   [*Exit*, L.

SIR H. My dear madam, you must perceive this unfortunate occurrence was no fault of mine. I was compelled to act as I have done—I was willing to offer any apology, but that resource was excluded as unacceptable.

LADY G. I know—I know—'twas I made him write that letter—there was no apology required—'twas I that apparently seduced you from the paths of propriety—'twas all a joke, and here is the end of it.

Enter MAX, SPANKER *and* DAZZLE, L.

Oh! if he had but lived to say, "I forgive you Gay!"

SPAN. So I do!

LADY G. (*seeing him*). Ah! he is alive!

SPAN. Of course I am!

LADY G. Ha! ha! ha! (*embraces him*) I will never hunt again—unless you wish it. Sell your stable——

SPAN. No, no—do what you like—say what you like for the future!

I find the head of a family has less ease and more responsibility than I, as a member, could have anticipated. I abdicate !

Enter COOL, L.

SIR H. Ah! Cool, here! (*aside to* COOL) You may destroy those papers—I have altered my mind, and I do not intend to elope at present. Where are they ?

COOL. As you seemed particular, Sir Harcourt, I sent them off to London by mail.

SIR H. Why, then, a full description of the whole affair will be published to-morrow.

COOL. Most irretrievably !

SIR H. You must post to town immediately, and stop the press.

COOL. Beg pardon—but they would see me hanged first, Sir Harcourt ; they don't frequently meet with such a profitable lie.

SERVANT (*without*). No, sir ! no, sir !

Enter SIMPSON, L.

SIMPSON. Sir, there's a gentleman, who calls himself Mr. Solomon Isaacs, insists upon following me up.   [*Exit*, L.

Enter MR. SOLOMON ISAACS, L.

ISAACS. Mr. Courtley, you will excuse my performance of a most disagreeable duty at any time, but more especially in such a manner. I must beg the honor of your company to town.

SIR H. What ! how ! what for ?

ISAACS. For debt, Sir Harcourt.

SIR H. Arrested ? impossible ! Here must be some mistake.

ISAACS. Not the slightest, sir. Judgment has been given in five cases, for the last three months ; but Mr. Courtley is an eel rather too nimble for my men. We have been on his track, and traced him down to this village, with Mr. Dazzle.

DAZ. Ah! Isaacs! how are you ?

ISAACS. Thank you, sir. (*speaks to* SIR HARCOURT.)

MAX. Do you know him ?

DAZ. Oh, intimately ! Distantly related to his family—same arms on our escutcheon—empty purse falling thro' a hole in a—pocket ; motto, " Requiescat in pace "—which means, " Let virtue be its own reward."

SIR H. (*to* ISAACS). Oh, I thought there was a mistake ! Know, to your misfortune, that Mr. Augustus Hamilton was the person you dogged to Oak Hall, between whom and my son a most remarkable likeness exists.

ISAACS. Ha ! ha ! Know, to your misfortune, Sir Harcourt, that Mr. Hamilton and Mr. Courtley are one and the same person !

SIR H. Charles !

YOUNG C. Concealment is in vain—I am Augustus Hamilton.

SIR H. Hang me if I didn't think it all along ! Oh you infernal cozening dog ! (*crosses to him*.)

ISAACS. Now, then, Mr. Hamilton——

GRACE. Stay, sir—Mr. Charles Courtley is under age—ask his father.

SIR II. Ahem !—I won't—I won't pay a shilling of the rascal's debts—not a sixpence !

GRACE. Then I will—you may retire.   [*Exit* ISAACS, L.

YOUNG C. I can now perceive the generous point of your conduct to-

wards me; and, believe me, I appreciate, and will endeavor to de-
serve it.

MAX. Ha! ha! Come, Sir Harcourt, you have been fairly beaten—
you must forgive him—say you will.

SIR H. So, sir, it appears you have been leading, covertly, an infernal town life?

YOUNG C. Yes, please, father. (*imitating* MASTER CHARLES.)

SIR H. None of your humbug, sir! (*aside*) He is my own son—how
could I expect him to keep out of the fire? (*aloud*) And you, Mr.
Cool!—have you been deceiving me?

COOL. Oh! Sir Harcourt, if *your* perception was played upon, how
could *I* be expected to see?   [*Exit*, L.

SIR H. Well, it would be useless to withhold my hand. There, boy!
(*he gives his hand to* YOUNG COURTLEY. GRACE *comes down on the
other side and offers her hand; he takes it*) What is all this? What
do you want?

YOUNG C. Your blessing, father.

GRACE. If you please, father.

SIR H. Oho! the mystery is being solved. So, so, you young scoundrel, you have been making love—under the rose.

LADY G. He learnt that from you, Sir Harcourt.

SIR H. Ahem! What would you do now, if I were to withhold my
consent?

GRACE. *Do* without it.

MAX The will says, if Grace marries any one but you, her property
reverts to your heir-apparent—and there he stands.

LADY G. Make a virtue of necessity.

SPAN. I married from inclination, and see how happy I am. And if
ever I have a son——

LADY G. Hush! Dolly, dear!

SIR H. Well! take her, boy! Although you are too young to marry.
                                        [*They retire with* MAX.

LADY G. Am I forgiven, Sir Harcourt?

SIR H. Ahem! Why—a—(*aside*) Have you really deceived me?

LADY G. Can you not see through this?

SIR H. And you still love me?

LADY G. As much as I ever did.

SIR H. (*is about to kiss her hand, when* SPANKER *interposes between*)
A very handsome ring indeed.

SPAN. Very. (*puts her arm in his and they go up.*)

SIR H. Poor little Spanker!

MAX. (*coming down, aside to* SIR HARCOURT). One point I wish to
have settled. Who is Mr. Dazzle?

SIR H. A relative of the Spankers, he told me.

MAX. Oh, no, a near connection of yours.

SIR H. Never saw him before I came down here, in all my life. (*to*
YOUNG COURTLEY) Charles, who is Mr. Dazzle?

YOUNG C. Dazzle, Dazzle—will you excuse an impertinent question?
—but who the deuce are you?

DAZ. Certainly; I have not the remotest idea.

ALL. How, sir?

DAZ. Simple question as you may think it, it would puzzle half the
world to answer. One thing I can vouch—Nature made me a gentleman—that is, I live on the best that can be procured for credit. I
never spend my own money when I can oblige a friend. I'm always
thick on the winning horse. I'm an epidemic on the trade of tailor.
For further particulars inquire of any sitting magistrate.

Sir H. And these are the deeds which attest your title to the name of gentleman? I perceive you have caught the infection of the present age. Charles, permit me, as your father, and you, sir, as his friend, to correct you on one point. Barefaced assurance is the vulgar substitute for gentlemanly ease; and there are many, who, by aping the *vices* of the great, imagine that they elevate themselves to the rank of those, whose faults alone they copy. No, sir! The title of gentleman is the only one *out* of any monarch's gift, yet within the reach of every peasant. It should be engrossed by *Truth*—stamped with *Honor*—sealed with *good-feeling*—signed *Man*—and enrolled in every true young English heart.

CURTAIN.

GET THE BEST!! GET THE BEST!!!

PRICE 10 CENTS EACH.

DE WITT'S "SCHOOL" SPEAKERS.

Neither talent, labor nor money have been spared in producing this series of books for youths. The result is that they excel all others both in quality and quantity of superior reading, while none others approach them in neat printing and general appearance. Nothing would warrant such an outlay but the enormous number sold, the price being only TEN CENTS *for each book.*

No. 1. DE WITT'S "PRIMARY" SCHOOL SPEAKER.
This book is made up entirely of short pieces. Each article is exactly fitted, both in ideas, sentiment and words, to interest, instruct and amuse the youngest reader and speaker. Every piece has been carefully garnered and winnowed from the best harvests of the best writers for youthful minds.

No. 2. DE WITT'S "PUBLIC" SCHOOL SPEAKER.
This work will be found well calculated for a grade of speakers a little more advanced than the "Primary." Many of the articles have been purposely written for these pages by authors of approved ability ; others carefully culled from the books of leading writers in either hemisphere. Care has been taken that every doubtful phrase and sentiment, however brilliant, should be eliminated from every line of this series.

No. 3. DE WITT'S "EXHIBITION" SCHOOL SPEAKER.
This work is for a grade of pupils still higher in intellect and learning than No. 2. The ideas and language are both more advanced, the selections being made with the intention of rendering the work just the thing to place in the hands of pupils desiring to recite in halls of Academies and other places of education. It has been successfully aimed in this book to instil worthy sentiments while aiding in the cultivation of the forensic powers.

No. 4. DE WITT'S "PATRIOTIC" SCHOOL SPEAKER.
The finest, most poetical, most ardent apostrophes to Home, Liberty, Union, Independence, will be found in this book. While specimens are given of the patriotic epics of other lands, our selections are mainly taken from the lyrics of our own great poets—poets who have poured out their burning phrases like molten lava streams, filling every American youth's heart with the idea

> "That the rude whirlwind and the torrent's roar
> But bind him to his *native* hills the more."

No. 5. DE WITT'S "DRAMATIC" SCHOOL SPEAKER.
This book furnishes a much needed collection of the most justly popular pieces in the language—pieces as remarkable for the purity of the sentiment as the chaste eloquence of the phrases. They are all characterized by strength, eloquence, and, in many instances, by grandeur of expression. All of the articles are eminently fitted for oratorical practice and display in Private as well as Public Schools, Academies and other institutions of education.

No. 6. DE WITT'S "COMIC" SCHOOL SPEAKER.
This most amusing book includes in its pages a great number of the best humorous pieces in the language. They are of all shades of fun, from the most delicate playfulness to the most broadly farcical, but all full of the very spirit of harmless jollity. While some of the pieces are those old standard recitations that never tire or stale by repetition, many others are full of the new, and fresh, and original humor of the times.

*** Single copies sent on receipt of price, postage free.

☞ Address as per first page of this Catalogue.

9 7 8 3 7 4 4 7 8 9 3 1 8